PASSOVER
The LAST SIX DAYS Of Jesus Life On Earth

Dr. Akiva Gamliel Belk

Founder:

jewishpath.org

B'nai Noach Torah Institute, LLC

bnti.us

Copyright © 2012

Dr. Akiva Gamliel Belk

All rights reserved.

ISBN-13: 978-0615639086

ISBN: 0615639089

Publisher
B'nai Noach Torah Institute, LLC
Post Office Box 14
Cedar Hill, Missouri 63016
talk@bnti.us
First Edition 02-28-2013

DEDICATION

I Made A Mistake!

I made a mistake by believing
what I was taught.

My parents impressed upon me
out of sin I was wrought.

Humankind could not survive
without a savior is what I got.

So, I believed that JESUS
of the Father was begot.

For years to this Jesus
I prayed and sought.

Eventually realizing
he was nothing more than a thought.

I made a mistake
and now I am distraught.
Look at all the mess

my actions have brought.

What shall I do with my aught?

I shall relax with myself and not be fraught.

I shall acknowledge
my mistakes of past naught.

I shall change my way
of living to pure, holy and taut...

This book is dedicated
to all who believed and fought

On the righteous path of life,
it was not for naught

PASSOVER, The LAST SIX DAYS Of Jesus Life On Earth

Table of Contents

DEDICATION..5
  I Made A Mistake!.....................................5
FORWARD..9
PREFACE...11
  How This Book Began..............................11
ACKNOWLEDGEMENTS.............................21
INTRODUCTION..29
Chapter One...39
  Let The Exploration Begin.......................39
Chapter 2...45
  How was time measured in the Gospels?.....45
Chapter 3...49
  Computers Influence................................49
Chapter 4...53
  Lunar Year / Solar Year............................53
Chapter 5...61
  When Does A Day Begin And End?..............61
Chapter 6...69

- How Is A Biblical Hour Measured?..................69
- Chapter 7...85
  - Chapter 8..95
  - Unleavened Bread..95
    - The Festival of Matzah..............................95
- Chapter 9...105
  - Preparation Day..105
- Chapter 10...113
  - Passover or Last Supper............................113
- Chapter 11...135
  - Let The Detour Begin.................................135
- Chapter 12...151
  - More Conflict With John.............................151
- Chapter 13...157
  - So What Really Happened?.......................157
- Index of Days For First Month.........................159
- References for Hebrew Scriptures..................187
- References for Christian Writings...................189
- About The Author..201
- Other Books By Dr. Akiva Gamliel Belk...........203

FORWARD

<u>The Last Six Days Of Jesus Life On Earth</u> written by my husband Dr. Akiva Gamliel Belk is an eye opener. It is filled with facts and references, which in some books are hard to find. Dr. Akiva Gamliel has taught on the internet for many years and has always required his students to provide accurate references for any issue, discussion or question. This eliminates hearsay providing a common place to start when addressing any issue. References are so very important for a book discussing such sensitive issues as these.

Many years ago as I studied the Bible, I began to formulate questions about some of the discrepancies I saw in the Christian Writings. I purchased and read everything I could find on the subject about the validity of the Christian Writings. My research eventually brought me to BNTI.us (B'nai Noach Torah Institute, LLC). This was paradise for me. Here I was able to find facts. Before coming to B'nai Noach Torah Institute, LLC it was a very difficult journey with limited study material. I studied at B'nai Noach

Torah Institute, LLC for several years, becoming acquainted with Dr. Akiva Gamliel. After years of study and reasoning as it says in Isaiah 1.18, *Come now, and let us reason together, Saith the LORD.* I left Christianity and returned to the faith of my Mother's Family, Judaism. A journey like this requires courage and tenacity. It can be a very arduous journey as well.

If uncovering the truth for oneself and finding a Loving, Kind, Gentle and Caring Creator is a journey you want to take, then put aside all that you have been taught and read this book. Don't make any decisions as your read. Wait, think about what you are reading. Search your own books, the Internet and see if the facts in this book hold up under your own research. They will! I have Christianity to thank for teaching me to believe in God and for carrying me through many tough experiences. I have Judaism to thank for providing me the correct way to live.

Rebbetzin Brachah Rivkah 'Revi' Belk

PREFACE

How This Book Began

It was a bright sunlit day in the small industrial town of Sheridan Colorado back in the late 1980's. Sheridan was a poorer town surrounded by the wealth of Littleton to the east, Englewood to the west, smaller homes of Denver to the north and a recently built nearly vacant bankrupt shopping mall next to open fields with cattle grazing to the south. At that time of the morning there was little traffic on the four-lane highway in front of our family printing business. Down the highway to the north the freeway in the valley was busy with traffic. The businesses directly south were closed. The small police station and town hall appeared asleep with a few police cars parked out front in angled parking spaces near the street. Sheridan was one of those small unimportant towns where big wealthy influential cities placed mental health facilities, half way houses and other types of businesses and facilities unwanted in their neighborhoods. The elementary school that our youngest son, Joel attended, was a block and a half up the street to the west. The middle school our older son, Joshua attended, was several blocks down the street to the north.

Looking back, that day seemed pleasant. It was like so many other similar days. It seemed uneventful. The sun cheerfully shone through the large plate glass windows lighting up the lobby of our print shop, as it often did. The lobby had that good clean warm feeling when customers entered.

What set this day apart from others was a visit from a Baptist preacher named Grady. He did something that really upset me. He talked disparagingly about this 'poor tiny Independent Fundamental Baptist Church' down the way. I had no idea that it existed until he came in. I thought he was brazen about what he intended to do. He was courting the board… He was politicking the membership… He was so confident of his impending election as Pastor that he ordered costly business cards with the church name, his name as Pastor, the address, phone number and a spiffy cliché even before the church board had called for an election.

About now readers should be wondering what does all this have to do with <u>The Last Six Days of Jesus Life</u>. Well, if it had not have been for good old brother Grady visiting that day and ordering those business cards I would have not got all wound up inside. I purposed in my heart right then and there while Grady was ordering those cards to visit that poor little memberless Baptist church several miles away. And wouldn't you know it, before the preacher left, he gave a special invitation to me, my wife at that time, Lanie, and our boys to come to services at the Baptist Church. He included directions and times of services.. Looking back, perhaps I gave the appearance of a man desiring a warm church home.

Later that day I mentioned to Lanie that I felt the need for our family to visit this Baptist church on Wednesday night. That went over like a sack of rocks in your salad. In those days it was pretty much unheard of for a new family to visit an out of the way church on a Wednesday night for

Bible Study. Look, I understand she was tired. She worked long and hard at the office then at home. A woman's work is never done. There is this daily cycle of breakfast, lunch and dinner. There is this weekly cycle of clean the bathrooms, sweep and mop the floors and do the laundry. There is a lot more... So, I understand why it did not go over well. Men, our wives need time to spend doing some things that are fun. They need some down time. Ladies need time to do other things.

Well, when we showed up the preacher was there along with the two remaining deacons, their wives and a few other members. We received a lot of attention. The four of us almost doubled the size of those in attendance that evening. Then the preacher announced that he met us earlier in the week and had invited us. That went over very well. This more or less gave the impression that this Preacher was out doing the work of the Lord and trying to build this little church he expected to be elected Pastor to.

The service began with prayer then the more

senior of the two elder Deacons led the song service. I don't remember if Lanie played the piano that evening or not. Most of us sang out of key. It was pretty rough. I felt a little sorry for the boys. Next they took up the offering. We contributed. I don't remember if we wrote a check or dropped a bill. After the offering the preacher taught. For some reason he got all wrapped up in secular humanism and we had a bit of a tangle almost from the onset. It was his opinion that there was no definite right or wrong that everything depended upon the circumstances. I just could not swallow what he was saying.

After the service the Deacons and their wives shook our hands and spent a few minutes getting acquainted. The elderly deacons were warm, friendly and curious. I shared that we owned a family printing business up the street. Perhaps Lanie may have had a premonition of what was about to happen... I cannot speak for her... I invited Deacons to visit our business at their leisure.

Either the next day or the following day the senior

Deacon came by for a visit. He was a distinguished looking man with white hair and a very deep voice. He came by to say they appreciated us visiting and he hoped we would come often. I assured him we would visit again, even though, in the back of my mind I could imagine this may not go over well with the rest of the family.

When the Deacon visited, wouldn't you know it, he was curious about how we knew Preacher Grady. He was surprised to learn we met a few days prior when he stopped by to order business cards. Those cards were sitting on a table close to the counter along with other orders. The Deacon wanted to have a look. Several days before one of us called and informed Preacher Grady that his cards were printed and ready for pick up. Was it our fault that Preacher Grady had not stopped by to pay for his business cards and to pick them up? After all, what are business cards for? They are to show and to hand out.

I turned away from the counter where the Elderly Deacon stood. I reached over and picked up the box of business cards from the table then turned back again. I set the business cards on the counter. He picked up the box and stared at the cards. Wow! Was he surprised! He was really taken back. His eyes almost popped out of his head. He wanted to know more about the business cards. He informed me that Grady was not the Pastor yet and that the church had not even scheduled a church membership meeting to even discuss the matter. We talked a while. Perhaps, I may have shared a little more than was necessary. He learned that I was a former Pastor of a successful church near downtown Denver and that I had attended Bible College and Seminary in California and Colorado and that I had a Doctorate in Theology. I did not share anything about me being Jewish. Needless to say Preacher Grady was not elected. However, in short order I was. This is a story for another book. All I am doing is setting the stage of how I began to write this book.

The examination of Jesus last six days on earth began over twenty years ago when as the Pastor of that Baptist church I thought it would be exciting to share with the Congregation a scholarly examination of Jesus last six days on earth in a chronological journey leading up to Passover and then on to the death of Jesus. So I began studying months in advance to make sure that there would be plenty of time before Easter to share on this interesting subject.

I was not prepared for the events that would unfold as my studies began to develop. What you are about to read is a true story taken from a few pages of my life. Instead of revealing more now let's begin the Journey together so that you may be able to share what I experienced. I would enjoy hearing from you after absorbing the fullness of these experiences.

Having said this, I strongly encourage anyone who is not familiar with The Torah, or with Judaism or with Passover to prepare some. Even though I have labored to make this book understandable, yet, there are so many built in confusions within the Christian Writings by various religions that will challenge any reader of this book. I stopped the publication of this book for a year because of the confusion other religions have woven in to the Christian Writings. During this year I wrote two books to help deal with that confusion. The first book is entitled, Would You Like to be Jewish? The second book is, Would You Like To Be Jewish 2 ? One of the purposes for writing these two books was to show how other religions double talk, introduce confusion, misunderstandings and sow disinformation about Judaism and The Torah Portion of the Bible. The confusion is deliberate!!

ACKNOWLEDGEMENTS

My parents have gone on to the next life, may they rest in peace. May their memory be for good! At the time of their departing they would not have approved of the discussion in this book. Still, they are my parents and I love them both very much. Even when parents strongly disagreed with their children and children with their parents they are to be honored because they gave us life. They are our precious parents

I also greatly appreciate my grandparents who I learned about through family members. My father was an orphan from the age of five. My mother was forced to live a great distance from her parents, so for a grandchild living over a thousand miles away, getting to know ones grandparents was difficult.

We visited relatives just a few times when I was growing up. My father did not want the influence of my mother's relatives in our lives. They did not care much for Daddy either. My grandparents spoke several languages. When Daddy came around they did not speak much in English. They shut him out. Daddy forbid the use of any language in our home but English. He considered it disrespectful to the Holy Ghost. When I entered the fifth grade our class began to learn Spanish. Daddy forbid it. He went to the elementary school to protest. The Principle set him straight. A Czechoslovakian family moved in up the street from us. I began to learn their language. Daddy found out. He put a stop to it. There are many individuals like my father that don't understand. Sometimes, what they do not understand scares them. In addition to this they maybe a bit narrow minded. I understand this. Daddy kept us a fair distance from our relatives.

I remember several of the driving trips in our Pontiac station wagon from Colorado to Illinois and back. Daddy and Momma would put the seats down in the back of the station wagon. They would place several sleeping bags, sheets, blankets, pillows etc. in the back of the station wagon. In back of the station wagon in one corner Daddy would put this red metal old time coca cola ice box. He would place a huge block of Ice in the ice box along with some grape and orange soda pop, 7up and Squirt. Momma liked 7up. Daddy liked Squirt. My two brothers and I liked the grape and orange soda pop.

All the bottles were glass. In those days we were charged between two pennies and a nickel deposit for each bottle. My younger brothers and I were big time pop bottle collectors, kids could buy a lot with a nickel.

The ice box had an upper chamber that lifted out where we kept sandwich meat, mayonnaise, mustard, tomato slices, lettuce etc. On the other side directly across from the red ice box were several paper bags with bread, Red Seal Potato Chips, paper plates, napkins and some plastic forks, knives and spoons.

Those road trips were long and boring. There were no interstates. Gas stations, also known as Filling stations and Service stations were small and long distances apart. They were not like the QT's Stations of the 21st Century. They would normally have dirty bathrooms with filthy sinks.

There was writing everywhere. The stations normally had several service bays for auto work. Sometimes there would be a soda machine where for a nickel or dime one could buy an Orange Crush or a Grape Duffy or a Pepsi or Coke. The people that ran the Service stations had employees that would pump your gas, wash your car windows, whisk broom or vacuum out the floor areas of the car. They would check your oil and tires etc. In those days people drove with their windows down. Air conditioning as we know it did not exist. Most cars had a column shift and did not have automatic transmissions, power steering or electric windows. We were lucky to have an AM radio let alone an AM, FM1 and FM2 with DVD and surround stereo sound. Tinted windows and sky lights were not invented. The point is that traveling was different than today.

My brothers and I took turns *running the soda machine*. Those were the days. Wow!

Growing up under a father that was strict and demanding was difficult. Yet, the Bible Instructs us in,

Exodus 20.12.
Honor your father and your mother so that your days may be long upon the land which the Lord our God Gives you.

We would be driving down the road and Daddy and Momma would start praying, It could get quite intense for five or ten minutes. You just never knew what to expect...

My wife, Brachah Rivkah lost both her father and mother prior to our late in life marriage. Yet, somehow, I feel like I know them through pictures and stories Revi and other relatives have shared with me. Revi's Father was a man who read the Bible but did not enjoy going to congregation. At one time he wanted to purchase the Temple in Cape Girardeau, Missouri for Revi to have a place to worship. It's closed now. It was vacant and for sale because many of the Jewish families moved. Even though he would not attend himself he wanted a place of worship for his daughter. God Bless him! Revi's Mother was pretty stern with her. Revi's life was difficult. For many years there was this demilitarize war zone between the two of them.   Then one day the Creator Impressed upon Revi to just forgive her mother for all the challenging times when they were at odds. Revi did this and they united and enjoyed each other during the last years of her life.

Revi and I are most thankful for our parents. This book is dedicated to our parents. May they rest in peace.

We each have parents. They are not perfect. We must allow some space for each of our failings.

We have the very special honor to still enjoy the presence of Revi's step-mother, Katy. She is so very special. We both love her so much and desire to spend as much time as we can together. Katy comes to visit us every once and a while for a week or two. We visit Katy also. We receive so much pleasure from our time together. Katy leads an active life doing things many ladies would not attempt. We appreciative this righteous lady who fills our lives with knowledge, care, direction and so many blessings.   Katy reads the books we publish and reviews every page lovingly with Revi me. I say this because, we are each individuals and see life a bit differently. Thank God that does not stop the love and compassion we share between us, Kaw Naw Nah Hah Raw.

Katy read this book. It did not pass. I had to rewrite it.

Dear Reader I have been studying the Biblical measurement of time for decades. In the pages that follow you will see it is complicated. I acknowledge that it is a great challenge to understand. Yet, I have labored much to make the pages of this book easy to understand and to bring them alive with the truth and some stories.
I ask that you do your best to follow the discussions on the measurement of time. It is so very important to being able to follow the chronology of the last six days of Jesus life on earth. Again I want to thank Katy. Much of the improvement in this book is due to her influence. We love you!

Thank you Katy!

INTRODUCTION

Dear Reader this is the second book in the Passover Series. The First was entitled, A Sincere Journey Ends Without JESUS.

In this book we are going to point out many places of disinformation. Some of this disinformation is intentional in my opinion. We are going to explain why the time period around Passover is so confusing. We are going to point out a number of inconsistencies between the Gospel Writers. We will observe that their writings are NOT in harmony.

One of the areas of confusion is in how time is measured in the Christian Writings. There is the traditional measurement of time according to the Hebrew Scriptures and then there is the time introduced by Pope Gregory XIII in 1582/5342 From Creation known as the Gregorian Calendar. The measurement of time in the Christian Writings is according to the Hebrew Scriptures. However today, 432 years from when the Gregorian Calendar originated most individuals know very little about how time is measured according to the Hebrew Scriptures. Come on... Why would anyone living in the 21 century want to learn how to measure time according to the Hebrew Scriptures? This confusion is complemented by almost three dozen different measurements of time. Yet, originally there was only one measurement of time. This one measurement is still used today. What is the purpose of the other calendars and their measurement of time? CONFUSION! Listen! There are over 730 religions in the world today. Is this progress? These religions have thousands of splinters into additional religions... Why is this so important?

Dear reader we are going to be measuring Jesus last week on earth chronologically. This can only be accurately done using the Hebrew Scripture's method of measurement. As we journey, the time issue will become obvious. One can overcome it but it is a challenge. Ask yourself - Do I want to know the Truth? How valuable is the Truth to me?

In Chapter One we begin with the goal I have for this book. I write, regardless of the conclusion we may each reach after reading <u>The Last Six Days of Jesus Life</u> my desire is that our journey should flow with interesting information and be filled with the richness of Jewish Passover Observances. It will be more authentic for the reader if I can help you to experience the thoughts and the struggles I felt.

We list a few rules this book will follow in the examination of Jesus Last six days on earth. Then I admit that twenty years ago my beliefs were biased in favor of Christianity. That is where I was then. This is where the story begins. Today I have returned to Judaism and try to live an observant life.

Chapter Two is a brief look at Biblical dates and times. They tell us when the Festival of Passover or the Festival of Unleavened Bread begin. They inform us if the day is Sabbath or a High Holiday. Sometimes they inform us of the day, the week or the month. We conclude that the Christian Writings were written using the same measurement of time as the Hebrew Scriptures. The changes in the measurement of time came about 1,500 years after the Christian Writings.

Chapter Three discusses the impact of modern technology, i.e. computers on Biblical research.

Chapters Four through Nine discuss the measurement of Biblical Time in eight different categories. We discuss and teach how time is measured by Year, by Month, by Day, by Night, by Hour, by Week, by Holy Days. In addition to this we compare two measurement systems for most of these categories. There is clearly a difference of opinion about how time is measured. I discuss three different theories. There is no way to adequately express in this introduction the importance of the measurement of time in the last six days of Jesus life on earth. This is why I divided each chapter into it's own category. This keeps our thoughts organized and easier to reference back to as one studies. I find it quite unique that the Gospel writers break the last day of Jesus life down into hours. This is quite rare. Yet it is fascinating and assists in establishing important points Christians have difficulty with.

In Chapter Seven we examine the use of the Sabbath Day, i.e. the Seventh Day as an anchor point to time measurement, time to and from, and as a time reference. Again there are those who argue that the use of the word Sabbath was in reference to Passover. Others teach that the use of the term Sabbath Day was in reference to both Sabbath and Passover. Then there are those that teach the use of Sabbath Day was in reference to the Seventh Day of the week, i.e. Sabbath. We discuss which position is correct and prove with references as to why it is correct. We dispute the other arguments.

Chapter Eight is another anchor in a chain of days that are established in the Hebrew Scriptures. On the fourteenth day of the month late in the afternoon is when the Passover Lamb is killed. Then a little later at nightfall is the beginning of the Passover Seder Meal. Both of these fall during the Festival of Matzah, i.e. Unleavened Bread. Then there is the Seventh

Day of Passover. Dear Reader once we establish a day and a date it is simply a matter of working back and forth. In addition Christians claim Jesus rode into Jerusalem on Sunday. They teach the crowd laid palm branches and garments in his path. They say this was his triumphant entry into the holy city.

In Chapter Nine we speak of Preparation Day as a point of time measurement and reference. Some argue that Preparation Day when used in the Gospels is in reference to Sabbath. Some argue Preparation Day is in reference to Passover. Others teach Preparation Day is in reference to both Sabbath and Passover. However once we establish the first day of the week as a day and time anchor, it is not difficult to work back from to prove which position is correct.

Chapter 10 is about John's statement that Jesus last meal was the [last] Supper. John states this was before the Passover Seder Meal. Matthew, Mark and Luke dispute John's position. We examine both positions to determine who is correct. There are some very clear issues with both positions.

Chapter Eleven is a 'Detour' where we take side streets so to speak to determine if John's position is correct. Come on! The Gospel writers say John was one of Jesus disciples for three years. Luke says John was one of those that went to prepare the Passover meal. Yet John says it was not the Passover meal it was a supper before Passover. This is an important date. This is the last meal with Jesus. That night Jesus is taken into custody by guards. The next day he is killed. Or is he? The point is that John should remember when it was. May individuals measure events in time from the death of a loved one. Is it possible John could have confused such an important event? Then we must ask, at that time, was Jesus death an important event? Maybe, the Catholic Church <u>has</u> made Jesus death an important event.

Chapter Twelve is entitled, <u>More Conflict With John</u>. Why? Most Bibles are 'Red Letter' editions. The red letters are supposed to be the very words Jesus spoke. People that love Jesus cling

to his words and to his quotes. Well based on what Jesus says in Matthew, Mark and Luke we have more conflicts with what John says.
Dear Reader, do you see the many angles of the last six days of Jesus life on earth?

Chapter Thirteen is what this book is all about. Chapter Thirteen is the chronological day by day account from the 8th Day of the First Month when Jesus came to Bethany through when Jesus died on the 15th Day of the First Month. The time frame is actually a little longer than six days. I include a chronological connection to every day and night referenced in the Gospels during this time frame. The reader will be able to follow the journey of Jesus from Bethany to the triumphant Entry to Jerusalem to the casting out of the money exchangers to the cursing of the fig tree to the preparation for the final Passover Seder Meal to the death and burial of Jesus to the first Day of the week.

Because I am Jewish and have a strong Christian past I share many helpful points that the non-Jewish world many be unaware of. Even though some Christian readers may be unhappy with points I make, each point is referenced so the reader can determine for her or his self what the truth is. The point of this book was and continues to be, a sincere examination of the last six days of Jesus life on earth. There is a great deal readers may learn from the time applications we discuss in this book. I have spent many years in preparing this book. God Willing another book dealing with controversial issues will follow this book. Originally I intended to included these as part of this book. They are important and interesting but need to be kept separate because they deal with other issues.

Chapter One

Let The Exploration Begin

Before beginning our exploration of the last six days of Jesus life there are several points to consider. Regardless of the conclusion we may each reach after reading <u>The Last Six Days of Jesus Life</u> my desire is that our journey should flow with interesting information and be filled with the richness of Jewish Passover Observances. It will be more authentic for the reader if I can help you to experience the thoughts and the struggles I felt. Slowly in a step-by-step way the Last Six Days Of JESUS life on Earth unfolded to me. I found myself asking unusual questions and having thoughts unaccustomed to me. Living through these experiences was both challenging and interesting. This book is a step-by-step guide through the last Six Days of JESUS Life on Earth. However it may not turn out just the way you would expect it to…

Whenever an individual attempts to do a scholarly examination, rules must be established and followed for others to follow.

Rule One is we are going to read and discuss the Gospels from a literal position. This step by step guide will go no where if we attempt to bend, ignore or rationalize away what is written in the Four Gospels.

Rule Two is we are going to examine written statements in the Gospels to determine their credibility. Is the statement truthful? Is the statement accurate? We are not considering the plausibility or feasibility or possibility of a statement. If a date and time can be measured we will measure it. Then the statement will be judged on the facts not the believability.

Rule Three is to be factual, to be objective, to be honest and to support all findings with references.

The Gospels will rise or fall based upon facts based upon what can be substantiated.

Dear Reader at the time I began this journey I was very biased even though this was not all that noticeable to me. I expect the exact same bias from you. That is OK!

Now, today my Christian bias of years ago is quite noticeable. That being the situation why should I expect anything different from the readers of this book. I expect the reader of this book to be a serious Christian with strong ties to their church, and to possess a dedication to weekly Bible study. That individual would own more than $10,000 in Christian books, commentaries, reference guides, Greek and Hebrew Bibles each with at least one interlinear, an encyclopedia, Bible dictionaries and on and on... In fact it would be necessary to set aside one room in the house or at the business to accommodate all the books just as I did. So if I were to say that a degree of bias did not exist that would be a complete falsehood. Yet at that time, twenty years ago I would not have thought of my beliefs as being biased. I was biased in favor of Christianity. That is where I was. Yet at that time I thought being neutral was an achievable goal. I was steeped in Christianity. My father was a Pastor of a successful congregation.

My father-in-law then was a former pastor. As a child I was raised to attend 9:30 AM Sunday School followed a 10:45 AM church service, a large family lunch, a short break then 6:00 PM youth service followed by 7:00 PM evening service. Then there was the middle of the week service and at times weeks of revival every night... There was visiting the sick, board meetings, teachers meetings, yearly conventions and on and on... Can you taste what it was like? Should I share about speaking in tongues and tarrying for the Holy Spirit in the prayer room for hours? We had a large prayer room off to the left of the platform in the front of the congregation. It is where people came to 'tarry for the Holy Spirit'. So dear reader if you are biased it's OK. If you are closed minded, its fine. If you enjoy hanging out with preacher types it's great. That is where I was at then...

I thought this exploration would be a fun Bible study with the congregation for a few weeks leading up to Passover. I thought the results were predictable. What could be so difficult about doing an examination of the last six days of

Jesus' life? If you feel this way then you are walking close to my steps.

As my journey began one of my goals was to see if it were possible to establish the day of the week with the date that the calendar event took place on according to the Gospel writers of the Christian Writings. This would help the congregation relate to the events better. One would think that linking days like Palm Sunday and Good Friday etc. with dates from the Christian Writings would be a snap. Actually this proved to be quite challenging. Can it be done? Yes! Another goal was to conclude this examination with a Friday evening Seder meal. Get the Congregation involved. We would have some type of reenactment of the Last Super. I would play the part of Jesus and members of the Congregation could play the parts of other interesting roles like Judas the trader, Doubting Thomas or Peter the stalwart. Later on in our Journey we will need to lean heavily on our rules and our goals. This never happened.

Chapter 2

How was time measured in the Gospels?

Are Biblical dates and times important? What purpose do dates and times serve?

Dear reader, Biblical dates and times tell us when the Festival of Passover or the Festival of Unleavened Bread begin. They inform us if the day is Sabbath or a High Holiday. Sometimes they inform us of the day, the week or the month. The writer Matthew makes more than 20 direct references to the Biblical dates and days during the last six days of Jesus life. Mark, Luke and John add another 38.

Matthew 4:12; 12:1; 12:40; 13:1; 15:32; 16:21; 17:1; 17:23; 20:19; 22:23; 26:2, **26:5**; 26:17; 26:61; 27:19; 27:40; 27:62; 27:63; 27:64; 28:1.

Mark 1:21; 2:23; 6:2; 9:31, 10:34; 12:12; 14:1; 14:12; 14:14: 14:16; 15:42; 16:2;

Luke 1:59; 2:41; 2:44; 4:16; 9:22; 13:16; 14:1;

22:1; 22:7; 22:8; 22:11; **23:43**; 23:56; 24:1;

John 1:39; 2:13; 2:23; 5:9; 6:4; 7:2; 10:22; 11:55; 12:1; 13:1; **18:28**; **19:14**

If dates, times and words were not important then why did the Gospel writers use them. The writer Matthew used these words to identify times and places for us the readers. In addition Matthew associates important events with the hour they occurred 14 times. Mark, Luke and John add an additional 13 references to the hour an event happened.

See:
Matthew 8:13; 9:22; 10:19; 15:28; 17:18; 20:3; 20:5; 20:6; 20:12; 24:36; 24:44; 26:55; 27:45,46.

Mark 13:35; 14:37; 14:41; 15:25; 15:33 - 35

Luke 12:39; 22:14; 23:44; 24:33

John 4:6; 19:14; **19:27**

We have the same right to use these times and

dates to support, dispute or challenge, if necessary.

I see no variation from the way time was measured in the Christian Writings, from how time was measured by Moses, Joshua, David etc. The Torah method of measurement of time is reinforced in the Christian Writings many times over. In the Christian Writings the Sabbath is always recognized as the Seventh Day. The High Holy Days are in their proper seasons. The measurement of hours in the Christian Writings was the same as thousands of years in the past.

Chapter 3

Computers Influence

We begin our journey by attempting to set a foundation for the days of the week each event occurred on. Connecting the day of the week with the date the event happened proved challenging.

If one thinks back to the time before computers became a very large part of our lives, research was approached quite differently than today. Around 1985 / 1986 Apple introduced the Mac Computer and later the Mac Plus Computer. That is when I became a computer person. This began opening up a brand new world of research for Biblical Scholars, Pastors, Congregation Leaders, Teachers etc. Our printing business purchased our first Mac. It was wonderful. Before long we owned several Macs. At that time few individuals would spend the $1,000.00 to $2,000.00 to own a Mac. Not only did we spend the money but we purchased software from retailers like Zondervan Books. We were, so to speak, on the cutting edge.

So if you were to go back with me to that time 27 years ago it would be necessary to own several Mac's to do the research. I sat at the company computer in the layout and design room of our printing business, which was about three miles from the Congregation I Pastored. I began the study of Jesus last six days on earth by laying out the four Gospels in four columns. I sat there thinking this is really cool. It's great to own a computer... Next when the feeling of satisfaction eventually calmed, I began searching for a date in the Gospels leading up to Passover that I could connect with the Torah portion of the Bible, (Genesis, Exodus, Leviticus & Deuteronomy). It had to be a firm clear reliable date that others would be able to see, understand and agree with.

Establishing dates with days was very important so I struggled with this for a while. Why? We have Christian days associated with the Jewish Celebrations of Passover. The Jewish calendar is based upon a lunar cycle. Guess what? Christians also follow the lunar calendar to a degree. Christians observe Easter around the same time Jews Observe Passover. I encourage the reader to study this area in a little more depth. So let's acquaint ourselves with how the Biblical calendar / the lunar calendar functions.

Chapter 4

Lunar Year / Solar Year

The Torah portion of the Bible Teaches we are to measure our time by the sun, moon and stars. So it is proper to measure accordingly.

Genesis 1.14
And God Said, Let there be lights in the firmament of the Heaven to divide the day from the night; and let them be for signs, and for seasons, and for days, and years...

Judaism measures time several ways. We measure years F.C., i.e. From Creation.

Catholics and Christians for the past 431 years have been measuring time in terms of years from when they estimate Jesus was conceived. This would be from around 3760 F.C. From 3760 F.C. Christians measure back using B.C. Or measure forward using A.D. There is no zero year. Jews contribute to the confusion of this system of measurement by using BCE instead of BC and

CE instead of AD. Our Creator confused the languages and we have confused just about everything else. For the most part, this paragraph will not be a part of the discussion.

A Lunar month in the Bible is the time between two new moons. A new moon is reached when the moon is closest to the Sun. A new moon is the first visible crescent of the moon after conjunction with the sun.. In terms of time a lunar month is 29 days, 12 hours and 44 minutes. A Lunar month consists of either 29 or 30 days.

In Judaism we are to Sanctify the moon. This is called, Kiddush Levanah. We say special prayers and blessings one evening, normally after Sabbath has past. We say these blessings outside of the synagogue when when we can view the moon. One may Sanctify the moon in individual prayer but it is best to do so in a minyan, i.e. with ten Jewish men above the age of twelve.

On one occasion I was saying Kiddush Levanah at our Colorado mountain home which was close to a forest area. As I was saying the prayers a conversation with a local businessman slipped into my mind. He told me that he saw two mountain lions chasing deer on the street in front of our home around 11:00 at night. Can you imagine what it is like to Sanctify the moon knowing a mountain Lion might be near by?

Dear Reader the point is that where ever Jews are, we are required to Observe Kiddush Levanah. This is a very important Observance because Kiddush Levanah was the first Observance given to the Children of Israel. Rabbi Moshe Weissman, The Midrash Says (Brooklyn, New York: Benei Yakov Publications 1980), p. 89.

Our Sages Teach that on the First Day of the First Month that the Lord Said,

Exodus 12.1
And the Lord spake unto Moses and Aaron in the land of Egypt, saying, This month shall be unto you the beginning of months: it shall be the First Month of the year to you.

From this our Sages Teach that we should go out to meet the New Moon, i.e the New Month. Rabbi Yochanan taught that one who goes out to Bless the New Moon in its proper time is like one who greets God's Presence, i.e. the Shechinah. The second purpose has to do with the Jewish People's rebirth... The Jewish people in Egypt were in decline just as the moon is once a month. Then as the moon is reborn from it's lowest point so are the Jewish people reborn. Rabbi Menachem Davis, The Shottenstein Edition Interlinear Chumash Bereishis / Genesis, {Brooklyn, New York: Mesorah Publications, Ltd. First Edition 1st impression 2007}, p 454. So on one hand we are Obligated to observe our year according to the Lunar year and on the other hand we realize the Spirituality that this Observance brings.

After all the years of being slaves and worshiping Egyptian idols we did not deserve to be redeemed. However, by our observing Kiddush Levanah at the proper time, on the First Month of the New Year in Egypt, and by our proper observance of taking, killing and placing the blood of the Pesach Lamb, and by roasting it outside we deserved to be delivered.

Rabbi Yochanan taught that Whoever pronounces the Blessings over the new moon in its due time welcomes, as it were, the Presence of the Shechinah... Rabbi Ishmael taught: Had Israel inherited no other privilege than to greet the Presence of their Heavenly Father once a month, it were sufficient, Sanhedrin 42 a.

A lunar year is about 354 days.

A solar month in terms of time is 30 days, 10 hours, 29 minutes, 3.8 seconds. A solar month is defined by the Gregorian calendar into 12 divisions that are either 28 days, 29 days, 30 or 31 days in length.

A solar year is about 365 days.

Dear Reader the Hebrew Scriptures follow the lunar year cycle within the solar year cycle. This results in a difference of 11 days between the lunar year (354 days) and the solar year (365 days). This does not have an impact on our discussion in this book so there is no need to go further on this subject.

Exodus 13.4-5.
On this day [the 15th Day of the 1st Month] you came out [of Egypt], in the month of spring. When the Lord brings you into the land of the Canaanites, and the Hittites, and the Amorites, and the Hivites, and the Jebusites, which he swore to do to your fathers, {He swore] to give you, a land flowing with milk and honey, as a result you shall keep this service [of Passover] in this month.

The seasons spring, summer, fall and winter follow the solar calendar. Dear One this is how our Creator designed the world to function.

However, if Jews were to observe Passover according to the lunar calendar alone Passover would change about ten days every year and eventually after 33 years return to the original date. This presents a problem. Why? Our Creator requires that Passover be Observed in the spring of every year as noted in Exodus 13.4,5

From this we understand that the season for Passover must always be in the springtime. This Observance stabilizes the Jewish calendar. This Command keeps all Biblical dates in the same time frame. We also learn that the Creator Commanded that this Month would begin the Jewish Religious cycle for the year. Our Creator Requires us to keep Passover as a spring Observance. This prevents Passover from cycling on and on for 33 years and eventually ending up back where the Observance originally began. Yet, on the other hand we do not follow the solar year. Passover is NOT on the same solar day each year like Independence Day each 4th of July. Passover begins on the same Lunar day each year. Passover begins late in the afternoon of the 14th day of the first Jewish Month each year.

Exodus 12.1-2.
And the Lord Spoke to Moses and to Aaron [while they were] in the land of Egypt, He Said,

This month shall be to you the beginning of months: it shall be the first month of the year to you.

So this separated the secular year. i.e. the solar year which is measured from Creation, from the religious year, the lunar year which is measured from spring. Christians don't count the annual cycle the same as in Judaism.

Chapter 5

When Does A Day Begin And End?

The Biblical day begins with nightfall one evening and ends with nightfall the next evening. How do we know this?

Genesis 1.5
... the evening and the morning were Day One.

Genesis 1.8
... the evening and the morning were the Second Day.

Genesis 1.13
... the evening and the morning were the Third Day.

Genesis 1.19
... the evening and the morning were the Fourth Day.

Genesis 1.23

...the evening and the morning were the Fifth day.

Genesis 1.31
...the evening and the morning were the Sixth day.

The Christian writers understood a day began at evening. This can be seen by John's comment.

John 20:1
On the first day of the week Mary Magdalene came to the tomb while it was early, when it was yet dark, and saw the stone taken away from the sepulcher.

The first day of the week had already begun. It was still dark. The sun had not risen. The first day of the week began at nightfall after Saturday day. It was termed *'the first day'* and *'it was yet dark'*. The sun had not come up. This explanation clarifies that there was no disagreement about how a day was defined until 431 years ago when Pope Gregory XIII introduced the Gregorian Calendar. The

Gregorian Calendar begins and ends a day at 12:00 am. It is NOT in the mid of night. The mid of night varies according to the time of the year.

Dear Ones, understanding when a day begins and ends in the Bible is very important in relation to the six days leading up to Jesus' death. We will come and go from this point many times in this book. One can see the confusion between the Biblical measurement from that of the Gregorian measurement. The Biblical measurement points to God who Created the world in six days / time periods. When one was making an appointment one would have to return to God's point of reference. The Biblical measurement kept God in our life as a focal point.

Matthew 21:18
Now in the morning as he returned into the city, he hungered.

This was the early morning. This was around the break of day. Jesus was traveling to the Temple for Morning prayers. This is a custom that is thousands of years old. This is what Jewish men did. They went to the Holy Temple or there synagogue first thing in the morning for morning prayers. While at the Temple the Levites would sing one of Seven Psalms. Rabbi Menachem Davis, Editor, The Shottenstein Edition Siddur for Weekdays, (Brooklyn, NY: Mesorah Publications, Ltd., First Edition, 2002), p 232

On the first day of the week the Levites sang Psalm 24

On the second day of the week the Levites sang Psalm 48

On the third day of the week the Levites sang Psalm 82

On the fourth day of the week the Levites sang Psalm 94.1 – 95.3

On the fifth day of the week the Levites sang Psalm 81

On the Sixth day of the week the Levites sang Psalm 93

On the Seventh day of the week, i.e. Sabbath the Levites sang Psalm 92

This was a way in which days were distinguished between each other. Each day is measured by it's own individual number.

Sunday is the First Day of the Week
Monday is the Second Day of the Week
Tuesday is the Third Day of the Week
Wednesday is the Fourth Day of the Week
Thursday is the Fifth Day of the Week
Friday is the Sixth Day of the Week
Saturday is the Seventh Day of the Week.

At the beginning of the final chapter of this book I share an example of what a Hebrew Calendar month looks like.

A month is measured from the first day to either the 29th or 30th Day.

Now a days the Sabbath, prior to the change from one month to another, is announced in the synagogue. Several thousand years ago they were dependent on witnesses that watched the moon to announce a new moon. The witnesses may or may not have been reliable. The changing of the new moon could have been hampered by cloud cover etc.

So if for example we were to read in the Christian Writings that in two days is the Festival of Unleavened Bread it is based upon at least three calendar measurements, i.e the measurement of the day in relation to the week, the measurement of the month in relationship to the year and the relationship of the day in relationship to the month.

Passover is the First Month of the religious New Year for the Children of Israel. Passover begins on the afternoon of the 14th day of the first month. Passover begins on Thursday, the Fifth Day of the week. The Festival of Unleavened Bread begins at night fall on the 15th Day of the First Month which is the beginning of the Sixth Day of the Week, Thursday night.

Matthew 26:17
Now the first day of the feast of unleavened bread the disciples came to Jesus, saying unto him, Where wilt thou that we prepare for thee to eat the passover?

The disciples knew this was the 14th day of the first month. They knew this day was Thursday, the fifth day of the week.

Matthew 26:18
And he said, Go into the city to such a man, and say unto him, The Master saith, My time is at hand; I will keep the passover at your house with my disciples.

Note the words, 'Go into the city' Jesus and his disciples were not in Jerusalem when they asked this question. Matthew, Mark and Luke agree that Jesus was outside the city of Jerusalem.

Chapter 6

How Is A Biblical Hour Measured?

The Biblical hour is determined by dividing the length of daylight by twelve. The length of brevity of a Biblical day does not matter. A Biblical Day is $1/12^{th}$ of the entire daylight and a Biblical Night is $1/12^{th}$ of the darkness. If one were to measure a Biblical hour by minutes an hour could be as long as 75 minutes or as short as 45 minutes.

The Gregorian hour is based upon 60 minutes. There are 12 hours in a Gregorian day. Some of the 12 hours of daylight, when days are shorter in winter, will actually be in darkness. The daylight hours are shorter. Some of the 12 hours of darkness, when nights are shorter in summer, will actually be in daylight. The night time hours are shorter. Some of the 12 hours of daylight in summer will actually be longer than 12 hours. The daylight hours will exceed 12 hours. Some of the 12 hours of darkness in winter will actually be longer. The night time hours will exceed 12 hours.

I understand this is confusing. Pope Gregory XIII introduced this confusion into our lives. If one were to view the Christian Writing using the Gregorian day or the Gregorian hour instead of the Biblical day or hour the results would be quite different. The Gregorian measurement of time draws one into confusion.

We are going to review several examples of a Biblical hour.

If the length of our present daylight is fourteen 60 minute hours the Biblical measurement for this same time is 12 - 70 minute hours. The Biblical measurement of an hour expands and contracts within twelve hours. So an hour is rarely 60 minutes.

If the length of our present daylight is fourteen 60 minute hours in the Gregorian measurement of time an hour remains as sixty minutes. The hours of daylight expand or contract. A day is rarely 12 hours.

The Biblical measurement of a day is measured

by daylight. The Biblical measurement of night is measured by darkness. The Gregorian measurement of a day is 12 hours. The Gregorian measurement of a night is 12 hours.

A few years back, a business lady and I were supposed to meet at Denver's Eastside Kosher Deli for lunch. We set the appointment for around 11:00 am. We set the appointment somewhere between a few days to several weeks in advance. I arrived a few minutes before 11 am. Selected a booth and ordered a soft drink. After waiting about 15 minutes I began to wonder if it was the wrong day so I checked my day planner. Nope, it was today at 11am. I began to wonder what happened. Then I realized we had a time change and one of us failed to make the adjustment by moving the clock ahead an hour. Shortly my cell phone rang... This happens all the time when daylight savings begins and ends. What is the point? How does this relate to an hour thousands of years ago? I am told that Bartholomew Manfredi, and Italian clockmaker invented the first pocket watch in 1462. In 1670 and English clockmaker named William Clement is credited with the development of the Grandfather style clock. We know that sundials and water clocks were in use two thousand years ago. In fact many different forms of measuring time existed. The form that we are discussing, i.e. the measurement of an hour depended on being able to see the sun and the moon. How would one measure time two thousand years ago on a very cloudy day? How would one know what time to meet another? How would one set appointments? The writer Matthew shares a story he says Jesus told about a householder that needed laborers to work in his vineyard. The householder went out early in the morning to hire workers, then again at the third hour, the sixth hour, ninth hour and finally the eleventh hour of the day. They each worked to evening. The point is that morning and evening were the only exact points of measurement. There were other points of measurement. Animals are accustomed to eating at certain times and giving milk at certain times etc. Yet on a cloudy day these time measurements move. The point is that one could be off significantly in there measurement of an hour.

Seeing the difference between The Biblical measurement of time from that of the Gregorian measurement of time helps us to see and acknowledge differences exist. On the other hand, we may not understand how the Biblical measurement of time functions. God Willing, I am going to share how the Biblical measurement of time functions.

Example of 13.5 – 60 Minute Hours of Daylight

Biblical Measurement of an Hour	
12 – 52.5 min hours	12 – 67.5 min hours

Gregorian measurement of an hour	
10.5 – 60 min hours	13.5 – 60 min hours

60 min hour x 24 hours = 1,440 min.
Daylight Hours

60 min hour x 13.5 hours = 810 min
Biblical Hour = 67.5 min
Divide 810 min by 12 hours = 67.5 min
Night Time Hours
60 min hour x 10.5 hours = 630 min
Night Time Biblical Hour = 67.5 min
Divide 630 min by 12 hours = 52.5 min
810 min + 630 min = 1,440 min

A Biblical day is always twelve periods of daylight and twelve periods of night. The minutes of a Biblical hour increase or decrease but the number of hours always remain the same. The way we understand time today is considerably different than Biblical hours.

Let's consider a day that has 13.5 hours of daylight, i.e. sunlight. In our present system the sixth hour of the day is 6 A.M. Remember the Gregorian measurement for a day begins a midnight. So while the 6th hour is 6 am The Biblical measurement begins at daybreak. This means the Biblical 6th hour is actually 12:30 pm of the Gregorian hour. This means one has crossed over to the 12 hours of night time by 30 minutes. Remember it is 12:30 pm. The ninth hour of our day is 9 a.m. The Biblical 9th hour is actually 3:30 pm of the Gregorian hour. This is 3 hours and 30 minutes into the 12 hours of night time. Now let's review the chart on the next page.

If sunrise is around 6:30 A.M. and sunset is around 8:00 P.M. we have 13.5 of our present hours of daylight. As stated above 13.5 hours of daylight would equal 12 – 67.5 minute periods. If sunrise is at 6:30 a.m. the hours would breakdown as follows:

Biblical Day Begins at 6:30 am		6.5 hr
1st Hour	Add 67.5 min to 6:30 am = **7:37.5 am**	7:30 am
	Add 67.5 min to 7:37.5 am	

2nd Hour	(22.5 min + 45 min = 67.5 min) 22.5 min = 8:00 am + 45 min to 8:00 am = **8:45 am**	8:30 am
3rd Hour	Add 67.5 min to 8:45 am (15 min + 52.5 min = 67.5 min) 15 min = 9:00 am + 52.5 min to 9:00 am = **9:52.5 am**	9:30 am
4th Hour	Add 67.5 min to 9:52.5 am (7.5 min + 60 Min = 67.5 min) 7.5 min + 9:52.5 am = 10:00 am + 60 min to 10:00 am = **11:00 am**	10:30 am
5th Hour	Add 67.5 min to 11:00 am (60 min + 7.5 min = 67.5 min) 60 min + 11:00 am = 12:00 am +7.5 min to 12:00 am = 12:07.5 am	11:30 am

6th Hour	Add 67.5 min to 12:07.5 am (52.5 min + 15 min = 67.5 min) 52.5 min + 12:07.5 am = 1:00 pm +15 min to 1:00 pm = **1:15 pm**	12:30 pm
7th Hour	Add 67.5 min to 1:15 pm (45 min + 22.5 min = 67.5 min) 45 min + 1:15 pm = 2:00 pm + 22.5 min = **2:22.5 pm**	1:30 pm
8th Hour	Add 67.5 min to 2:22.5 pm (37.5 min + 30 min = 67.5 min) 37.5 Min + 2:22.5 pm = 3:00 pm + 30 min to 3:00 pm = **3:30 pm**	2:30 pm
9th Hour	Add 67.5 min to 3:30 pm (30 min + 37.5 min = 67.5 min) 30 min + 3:30 pm = 4:00 pm +37.5 min to 4:00 pm = **4:37.5 pm**	3:30 pm

10th Hour	Add 67.5 min to 4:37.5 pm (22.5 min + 45 min = 67.5 min) 22.5 Min + 4:37.5 = 5:00 pm + 45 min to 5:00 pm = **5:45 pm**	4:30 pm
11th Hour	Add 67.5 min to 5:45 pm (15 min + 52.5 min = 67.5 min) 15 min + 5:45 pm = 6:00 pm +52.5 min to 6:00 pm = **6:52.5 pm**	5:30 pm
12th Hour	Add 67.5 min to 6:52.5 pm (7.5 min + 60 min = 67.5 min) 7.5 min + 6:53.5 pm = 7:00 pm + 60 min to 7:00 pm = **8:00 pm**	6:30 pm
There is a 90 min difference between The Biblical measurement from that of Gregorian measurement.		

Dear reader just as I have shown the the Biblical measurement for a day, there is a Biblical measurement for night. This example shows how different our present time and hour is from Biblical time. Let's apply this to the times provided in the Christian Writings by the Gospel writers to make this more meaningful. This will help us in our exploration to understand the corresponding comments from Matthew, Mark, Luke and John and to clearly identity what they said was happening during that time frame over two thousand years ago.

The third hour would begin around 8:45 am and conclude at 9:52.5 am.

How did we arrive at this time?
1. We add the hours of daylight. The hours of daylight are 13.5.
2. We multiply 13.5 hours times 60 minutes to = 810 minutes.
3. We divide the 810 minutes by 12 to tell us the length of a Biblical hour = 67.5.
4. Then we begin with the time the daylight hour begins. In our example day begins at 6:30 am.
5. We add three Biblical hours together, (67.5 + 67.5 + 67.5 = 202.5 minutes).
6. We add three 60 minute hours together (60 + 60 + 60 = 180).
7. Subtract 180 minutes from 202.5 minutes. This

leaves 22.5 minutes.
8. Next we add 3 hours to 6:30 am = 9:30 am + 22.5 minutes = 9:52.5 am.

Mark 15:25
And it was the third hour, and they crucified him.

The sixth hour is from 12:07.5 am to 1:15 pm. How did we arrive at this?
1. We add the hours of daylight. The hours of daylight are 13.5.
2. We multiply 13.5 hours times 60 minutes to = 810 minutes.
3. We divide the 810 minutes by 12 to tell us the length of a Biblical hour = 67.5.
4. Then we begin with the time the daylight hour begins. In our example day begins at 6:30 am.
5. We add six Biblical hours together, (67.5 min x 6 hours = 405 minutes).
6. We add six 60 minute hours together (60 minutes x 6 hours = 360 minutes).
7. Subtract 360 minutes from 405 minutes. This leaves 45 minutes.
8. Next we add 6 hours to 6:30 am = 12:30 pm + 45 minutes = 1:15 pm.

Matthew 27:45
Now, from the sixth hour there was darkness over all the land unto the ninth hour.

Mark 15:33
And when the sixth hour was come, there was darkness over the whole land until the ninth hour.

Luke 23:44
And it was about the sixth hour, and there was a darkness over all the earth until the ninth hour.

John has a little different recollection. He writes,

John 19:14
And it was the preparation of the Passover, and about the sixth hour: and he said to the Jews, Behold your King.

The ninth hour began at 3:30 pm to 4:37.5 pm
How did we arrive at this?
1. We add the hours of daylight. The hours of daylight are 13.5.
2. We multiply 13.5 hours times 60 minutes to = 810 minutes.

3. We divide the 810 minutes by 12 to tell us the length of a Biblical hour = 67.5.
4. Then we begin with the time the daylight hour begins. In our example day begins at 6:30 am.
5. We add nine Biblical hours together, (67.5 min x 9 hours = 607.5 minutes).
6. We add nine 60 minute hours together (60 minutes x 9 hours = 540 minutes).
7. Subtract 540 minutes from 607.5 minutes. This leaves 67.5 minutes or 1 hour and 7.5 minutes.
8. Next we add 9 hours to 6:30 am = 3:30 pm + 1 hour and 7.5 minutes = 4:37.5 pm.

Matthew 27:46 - 50
And about the ninth hour Jesus cried with a loud voice, saying, Eli, Eli, lama sabachthani? that is to say, My God, my God, why hast thou forsaken me? Some of them that stood there, when they heard that, said, This man calleth for Elias. And straightway one of them ran, and took a sponge, and filled it with vinegar, and put it on a reed, and gave him to drink. The rest said, Let be, let us see whether Elias will come to save him. **Jesus, when he had cried again with a loud voice, yielded up the ghost.**

It is during the ninth hour that Jesus dies.

Mark 15:34 - 37
And at the ninth hour Jesus cried with a loud voice, saying, Eloi, Eloi, lama sabachthani? which is, being interpreted, My God, my God, why hast thou forsaken me? And some of them that stood by, when they heard it, said, Behold, he calleth Elias. And one ran and filled a sponge full of vinegar, and put it on a reed, and gave him to drink, saying, Let alone; let us see whether Elias will come to take him down. And Jesus cried with a loud voice, and gave up the ghost.

Luke 23:44 - 46
And it was about the sixth hour, and there was a darkness over all the earth until the ninth hour. And the sun was darkened, and the veil of the temple was rent in the midst. And when Jesus had cried with a loud voice, he said, Father, into thy hands I commend my spirit: and having said thus, he gave up the ghost.

John 19:30
When Jesus therefore had received the vinegar,

he said, It is finished: and he bowed his head, and gave up the ghost.

The information in this chapter is very important. We will return to this many times through out this book.

Chapter 7

The Sabbath Day

The First Month of the Jewish New Year has a number of important dates. Several are associated with the Seventh Day, the Sabbath. As we examine events in a chronological order based on what the four writers of the Gospels have written we will do so in relationship to the Seventh Day. We will examine some of the events that unfolded during Jesus last week on earth in a time Measurement from Sabbath or to Sabbath. We are going to view what the Christian Writings say happened in light of the Torah portion of the Bible (Genesis, Exodus, Leviticus, Numbers and Deuteronomy) and we are going to see how days and times come together using the Seventh Day as a measurement. We can do this. Why? In the Torah portion of the Bible the Lord God Commands the Children of Israel to Observe the Sabbath. The Sabbath is the Seventh Day.

Genesis 2.2, 3

And on the Seventh Day God ended His work which He Had Made; and He Rested on the Seventh Day from all His work which He Had Made. And God BLESSED THE SEVENTH DAY, and Sanctified it; because that in it He Had Rested from all his work which God Created and Made.

Exodus 20.10, 11

But the Seventh Day is the Sabbath of the Lord your God; in it you shall not do any work, you, nor your son, nor your daughter, your manservant, nor your maidservant, nor your cattle, nor your stranger that is within your gates; For in six days the Lord Made Heaven and earth, the sea, and all that is in them, and rested the Seventh Day; therefore the Lord Blessed the Sabbath Day, and made it Holy.

The point is this. The Torah portion of the Bible establishes the Sabbath to be the Seventh Day of the week. As a result there will be times that we will use the Seventh Day as an anchor to measure forward or backward. The Seventh Day is an established time.

Days of the week are measured in their relationship to the Seventh Day. Six Days are intended for work. The Seventh Day is a Day when work ends and the Observance of Shabbat begins. The Biblical Sabbath begins eighteen minutes before sunset on Friday and ends the next evening after three stars appear in the sky.

There are two Sabbaths of great significance at the time of Passover. There is The Great Sabbath, which occurs the Sabbath before Passover. The Great Sabbath occurred on the Tenth Day of the First Month. The Great Shabbat during Jesus last six days on earth occurred on the day Christians call Palm Sunday. Then there was the Shabbat during Passover. During this Sabbath Jesus body lay in the tomb. Why do we call the one Sabbath the Great Sabbath? It is because in 2448 From Creation the Children of Israel did as our Creator Commanded. We took

those cute fuzzy white precious little lambs that we used to worship, and that the people of Egypt still worshipped, and marched down the streets. When they asked us what we were doing we said that we were going to kill their gods, place the blood from their gods on our doorposts and roast their gods in front of our homes in public to state we no longer worshipped them. We were repudiating our former Egyptian idol worship. We were making a statement that we now only Worship the Lord God of Israel. Our Sages teach that this very act was harder for the Egyptian people to bear than all the Plagues combined.
Rabbi Moshe Weissman, The Midrash Says (Brooklyn, New York: Benei Yakov Publications 1980), p. 60

It is interesting to note that the Great Sabbath fell on Sabbath during Jesus last six days on earth.

It is necessary to point out that the Gospel Writers distinguished between Sabbath, the Festival of Unleavened Bread and Passover. Matthew uses the Word Sabbath ten times, Mark eleven times, Luke eighteen times and John eleven times.

Matthew 12:1, 2, 5 (two), 8, 10, 11, 12; 24:20; 28:1

Mark 1:21; 2:23, 24, 27 (two), 28; 3:2, 4; 6:2; 15:42; 16:1

Luke 4:16, 31: 6:1, 2, 5, 6, 7, 9; 13:10, 14 (two), 15, 16; 14:1, 3, 5; 23:54, 56

John 5:9, 10, 16, 18; 7:22, 23 (two); 9:14, 16; 19:31 (two)

All four Gospel Writers agree that Jesus was dead in the grave over the Sabbath Day as noted below.

Matthew 28:1
In the end of the Sabbath, as it began to dawn toward **the first day of the week**, *came Mary Magdalene and the other Mary to see the sepulcher.*

Mark 16:1,2

And when the Sabbath was past, Mary Magdalene, and Mary the mother of James, and Salome, had bought sweet spices, that they might come and anoint him. And very early in the morning **the first day of the week**, *they came unto the sepulcher at the rising of the sun.*

Luke 23:50 – 24:1

And, behold, there was a man named Joseph, a counsellor; and he was a good man, and a just: (The same had not consented to the counsel and deed of them;) he was of Arimathea, a city of the Jews: who also himself waited for the kingdom of God. This man went unto Pilate, and begged the body of Jesus. And he took it down, and wrapped it in linen, and laid it in a sepulcher that was hewn in stone, wherein never man before was laid. **And that day was the preparation, and the Sabbath drew on.** *And the women also, which came with him from Galilee, followed after, and beheld the sepulcher, and how his body was laid. And they returned, and prepared spices and ointments; and* **rested the Sabbath day according to the Commandment. Now upon the first day**

of the week, *very early in the morning, they came unto the sepulcher, bringing the spices which they had prepared, and certain others with them.*

John 19:30 – 20:1
When Jesus therefore had received the vinegar, he said, It is finished: and he bowed his head, and gave up the ghost. The Jews therefore, because **it was the preparation, that the bodies should not remain upon the cross on the Sabbath day, (for that Sabbath day was an High Day,)** *besought Pilate that their legs might be broken, and that they might be taken away. Then came the soldiers, and brake the legs of the first, and of the other which was crucified with him. But when they came to Jesus, and saw that he was dead already, they brake not his legs: But one of the soldiers with a spear pierced his side, and forthwith came there out blood and water. And he that saw it, bare record, and his record is true: and he knows what he said was true, that you might believe. For these things were done, that the scripture should be fulfilled, A bone of him shall not be broken. And again*

another scripture saith, They shall look on him whom they pierced. And after this Joseph of Arimathea, being a disciple of Jesus, but secretly for fear of the Jews, besought Pilate that he might take away the body of Jesus: and Pilate gave him leave. He came therefore, and took the body of Jesus. And there came also Nicodemus, which at the first came to Jesus by night, and brought a mixture of myrrh and aloes, about an hundred pound weight. Then took they the body of Jesus, and wound it in linen clothes with the spices, as the manner of the Jews is to bury. Now in the place where he was crucified there was a garden; and in the garden a new sepulcher, wherein was never man yet laid. **There laid they Jesus therefore because of the Jews 'preparation day; for the sepulcher was nigh at hand.** *Then* **<u>on the first day of the week</u>** *Mary Magdalene came early, when it was yet dark, unto the sepulcher, and saw the stone taken away from the sepulcher.*

I included the lengthy texts to show that according to Luke Jesus died on Friday... Preparation Day... the sixth day of the week...

and was buried before Sabbath began at 8:00 pm and that Jesus followers rested on Saturday, the Sabbath Day, then early on the First Day of the week, i.e. Sunday they journeyed to the burial site of Jesus.

However John is a mess. John says Jesus ate a Supper, not the Passover Seder Meal and that Jesus died and was buried on the Preparation Day for Passover. This does NOT make any sense. We have two time lines. One time line begins on Friday, Six Days Before Passover. The Other Timeline begins at the opposite end Sunday the First Day of the week. John's account does not match. We will observe this later.

Now in addition to the First Day of the week we are also approaching the Seventh Day of Passover which begins on Tuesday Evening, the 21st Day of the First Month.

94

Chapter 8

Unleavened Bread
The Festival of Matzah

When we write of Unleavened Bread we are making reference to Bread that has no leaven, i.e. yeast. The bread is mixed with water, rolled out on a special protected table then perforated and baked all in less than 18 minutes to prevent any leavening.

Before the Children of Israel could enter into Passover, all their clothes, homes, sheds businesses, offices had to be leaven free. These are required Observances for the Children of Israel. This maybe where spring cleaning originated.

Exodus 12:14, 15
And this day shall be unto you for a memorial; and you shall keep it a Feast to the Lord throughout your generations; you shall keep it a Feast by an ordinance for ever. Seven days shall you eat unleavened bread; even from the First

day [of Observance] you shall put away leaven out of your houses: for whosoever eats leavened bread from the first day [of Observance] until the seventh day [of Observance], that soul shall be cut off from Israel. Outside of the Land of Israel, the Rabbis added an extra day of Observance.

Exodus 12.16,17
And in the First Day [Of Observance] there shall be an Holy Convocation, and in the Seventh Day [of Observance] there shall be an Holy Convocation to you; no manner of work shall be done in them, save that which every man must eat, that only may be done of you. And you shall observe the Feast of Unleavened Bread; for in this selfsame day have I brought your armies out of the land of Egypt: therefore shall ye Observe this day in your generations by an ordinance for ever.

Exodus 12.18 - 20
In the first month, on the fourteenth day of the month at even, you shall eat unleavened bread, until the one and twentieth day of the month at even. Seven days shall there be no leaven found

in your houses: for whosoever eats that which is leavened, even that soul shall be cut off from the Congregation of Israel, whether he be a stranger, or born in the land. You shall eat nothing leavened; in all your habitations shall ye eat Unleavened Bread.

Dear Ones, Passover and the Festival of Unleavened Bread run in conjunction with each other. The Christian Writers teach that Jesus and his disciples kept the Passover Seder and the Festival of Unleavened Bread.

Matthew, Mark and Luke agree that the Passover Seder Meal began at night fall on Thursday. John maintains that whenever the meal began, [on Tuesday] that it was the Last Super. If John were correct, and he is not, this would mean the Passover Seder Meal and Sabbath each were celebrated on the next night, i.e. Friday night. It is clear this did not happen based on a number of references between Matthew, Mark and Luke that we will shortly review.

What we are pointing out here, in this Chapter, is

that each Gospel Writer understood the difference between Sabbath, the Festival of Unleavened Bread and the Passover Seder Meal. Now, because many of our readers may not understand these celebrations I am including references. After all, why would readers who are not Jewish have any knowledge on the Observances of Sabbath, the Festival of Unleavened Bread and the Passover Seder Meal? It is not necessary to have an in depth understanding. Yet, it is important to know each Observance is required by our Creator for the Children of Israel. This means some of the narrative in the Gospels is wrong and at a later time in this book we will discuss this. If the Gospel narrative is correct , and it is not, it would require Jews living at that time to violate what God Commanded the Children of Israel to Observe. I can understand that this may not seem like that big of a deal. What is so new about the Children of Israel disobeying what God Has Commanded? I acknowledge this. It is true! Jews do not always do as our Creator Commands. Yet, based upon what I read in the Gospels, I have reason to believe most Jews

Observed what God Commanded. We shall see...

Dear Reader, God Willing, I am setting the stage so you will be able to have a greater knowledge of the Holidays and their required Observances.
To do this a we must set a little foundation in this chapter.

Numbers 28.16, 17
And in the fourteenth day of the first month is the Passover of the Lord. And in the fifteenth day of this month is **the feast:** *Seven Days shall Unleavened Bread be eaten.*

Here we learn that the Passover Lamb is killed on the fourteenth just before dark. Remember at nightfall the day changes. The Biblical time moves from the 14th to the 15th of the first month when the Seder meal is eaten and the miracles of Passover are told around the Seder Table in one's home. These Observances are part of the 613 Obligations I discuss in Book One entitled, Would You Like To Be Jewish? And in Book Two entitled, Would You Like To Be Jewish 2 ?

Matthew writes of the disciples preparing for the Passover Seder.

Matthew 26:17 - 20
Now the first day of the Feast of Unleavened bread the disciples came to Jesus, saying unto him, Where would you like us to prepare for you to eat the Passover [Seder]? And he said, Go into the city to such a man, and say unto him, The Master says, My time is at hand; I will keep the Passover at your house with my disciples. And the disciples did as Jesus had appointed them; and they made ready the passover. Now when the even was come, he sat down with the twelve.

Mark writes about the disciples desire to keep the Passover Seder and the Observance of Unleavened Bread.

Mark 14.1, 12
After two days was the Feast of the Passover, and of Unleavened Bread: and the chief priests and the scribes sought how they might take him by craft, and put him to death. But they said, Not

on the feast day, lest there be an uproar of the people.

Mark 14:12 – 17
*And the first day of unleavened bread, when they killed the passover, his disciples said unto him, Where wilt thou that we go and prepare that thou mayest eat the passover? 13 And he sendeth forth two of his disciples, and saith unto them, You go into the city, and there you shall meet a man bearing a pitcher of water: follow him. And wheresoever he shall go in, you should say to the goodman of the house, The Master says, Where is the guest chamber, where **I shall eat the Passover [Seder]** with my disciples? And he will show you a large upper room furnished and prepared: there make ready for us. And his disciples went forth, and they came to the city, and found the man as he had said to them: and they made ready the Passover [Seder]. And in the evening he came with the twelve.*

Luke wrote in greater detail about the Passover Seder meal and the Festival of Unleavened bread.

Luke 22:1, 7 -
Now the feast of unleavened bread drew nigh, which is called the Passover...

*Then came the day of Unleavened Bread, when the Passover must be killed. And he sent Peter and John, saying, Go and prepare for us the Passover [Seder] , that we may eat. And they said to him, Where do you want us to prepare? And he said to them, Behold, when you enter into the city, a man shall meet you bearing a pitcher of water; follow him into the house where he enters in. And you shall say to the goodman of the house, The Master says unto you, Where is the guest chamber, where I shall **eat the Passover with my disciples**? And he shall show you a large upper room furnished: there make ready. And they went, and found him as he had said to them: and they made ready the Passover. And when the hour was come, he sat down, and the twelve apostles with him. And he said to them, With desire **I have desired to eat this Passover with you** before I suffer:*

The Passover Lamb is killed late in the afternoon

of the 14th day of the month. The Passover lamb is killed in the Temple Court Yard. A Temple Priest caught the blood in a round cup and sprinkled the blood on the altar. Then the lamb or goat was hung up for skinning. After skinning the abdomen was cut open. The fatty portions were removed, salted and offered by a Temple Priest on the altar. The entrails were removed and cleaned. Remember more than one family could share the same lamb or goat. See the Jewish Encyclopedia for more information. That night was the first Passover Seder Meal. Six nights later would be the Seventh night. The 14th day is Passover. The 15th beginning with the night, is the Passover meal. The 16th at night is when we begin counting the Omer for 49 days. The Fiftieth Day is Shavuot, i.e. Pentecost. Then the 21st of the month begins the Seventh Day of Passover. Also during this time there is the Sabbath Preparation Day with Sabbath Day following.

Dear Reader, see how easy it is to become confused with so much going on. There are a lot of numbers and dates to absorb at Passover.

Chapter 9

Preparation Day

To best explain Sabbath Preparation, I would like to take a few pages from my book entitled, <u>Would You Like To Be Jewish?</u>

One evening I stopped by the home of a lovely couple. One of them opened the door and invited me in. When they turned on the hallway light, a Sabbath atmosphere engulfed me. You could say that I felt like a doughnut being dunked in my favorite coco. It was wonderful. The Sabbath Table was set. Everything was in it's special place. As I remember, the Sabbath Table was set with ornate silver candle holders with long twelve inch pure white tapered candles standing like flag poles high into the room. There was the silver kiddush plate and kiddush cup. Each were a handcrafted art piece. There was the Challah board and knife imported from Israel with a specially designed Challah cover. The crystal flower vase with a special Sabbath arrangement. The Sabbath table was set with the finest china and silverware. The napkins were hand crafted and pressed. The feeling of Sabbath was very, very powerful. They are examples of guarding the Sabbath.

My dear wife, Revi follows this same pattern, Kaw Naw Nah Hah Raw! The other night ago I was writing this book after dark. I took a break from writing just at the right time. Revi had just removed the Sabbath Challah. The Kitchen... dining... living room area and hallway were accented by the smell of fresh baked Challah loafs coming out of the oven. I walked over to view them. They were luscious. The Rebbetzin's homemade loafs looked like they were professionally baked. They were gorgeous! I got this strong Sabbath desire. I glanced over to the dining area to see Carrie bat Brachah Rivkah's Yahrzeit Candle glowing. There were three long stem red roses in a vase. The Sabbath Table was set with our best plates and silverware. Dear Reader, that does something to you. I commented to Revi about the Sabbath atmosphere. I felt in our home. It was exceptional, Kaw Naw Nah Haw Raw!

Dear Reader, since Sabbath is the time for cessation of work, the time for connecting with God one has to prepare in advance of Sabbath to make this possible and enjoyable. Sabbath has a meaning. Sabbath is intended to be a delight. Jews enjoy Sabbath candles... Sabbath table... Sabbath Kiddush, i.e. Challah and wine... Sabbath songs... Sabbath stories... Sabbath prayer... Sabbath learning... Sabbath walks... Sabbath nap... Yet the prep work is done before Sabbath.

Let's review what each writer says about the Preparation Day.

Matthew 27:59 – 62

And when Joseph had taken the body, he wrapped it in a clean linen cloth, And laid it in his own new tomb, which he had hewn out in the rock: and he rolled a great stone to the door of the sepulcher, and departed. And there was Mary Magdalene, and the other Mary, sitting over against the sepulcher. **Now, the next day, that followed the day of the preparation...**

Mark 15:42
And now when the even was come, because it was **the preparation, that is, the day before the Sabbath...**

Luke 23:52 - 54
This man went unto Pilate, and begged the body of Jesus. And he took it down, and wrapped it in linen, and laid it in a sepulcher that was hewn in stone, wherein never man before was laid. **And that day was the preparation, and the Sabbath drew on...**

Again, John maintains it was the Preparation for Passover. This differs with Matthew, Mark and Luke.

John 19.13, 14
When Pilate therefore heard that saying, he brought Jesus forth, and sat down in the judgment seat in a place that is called the Pavement, but in the Hebrew, Gabbatha. And it was the preparation of the Passover, and about the sixth hour: and he saith unto the Jews, Behold your King!

John 19:31, 42

The Jews therefore, because it was the preparation, that the bodies should not remain upon the cross on the Sabbath Day, (for that Sabbath day was an High Day,) besought Pilate that their legs might be broken, and that they might be taken away.

There laid they Jesus therefore because of the Jews 'preparation day; for the sepulcher was nigh at hand.

Here we read of a serious chronological difference between the Four Gospel Writers. Again, John states it was the Preparation for Passover. Is it possible John as the last Gospel Writer is setting the record straight. Matthew, Mark and Luke were already written. Maybe John was saying they were wrong. Yet, the issues / differences are not about a misuse of the terms. There is clearly a difference of opinion about what happened next. Our purpose in this chapter is to show the Writers understood the terms. They do. We will discuss the differences later.

Let's review the foundation we have tried to lay. We have just concluded discussing the measurement of Biblical Time in eight different categories. by Year, by Month, by Day, by Night, by Hour, by Day, by Week, by Holy Days. In addition to this we compared two measurement systems for most of these categories.

Dear Reader, now as we conclude the discussion on the measurement of Biblical time, you see first hand that it is complicated. I acknowledge that it is a great challenge to understand. When I began my study decades ago it was so confusing. I did not have a list of the eight different categories by which time is measured in the Bible. Actually there are more. No one explained to me the differences between the Biblical measurement from that of the Gregorian measurement. Maybe a scholar of greater understanding and communication skills will pick this book up and expand upon it clearer and in greater depth as needed.

Year -
Lunar Year

Solar Year

Month -
Lunar Month
Solar Month

Day -
The Measurement of A Biblical Day
The measurement of a Gregorian Day

Night -
The Measurement of A Biblical Night
The measurement of a Gregorian Night

Hour -
The Measurement of A Biblical Hour
The measurement of a Gregorian hour

Week -
Sabbath Day

Holy Days -
Unleavened Bread / The Festival of Matzah
Passover

Preparation -
Preparation Day for Sabbath…
Preparation Day for Passover…
Preparation Day for both Sabbath and Passover

Dear Reader, now we have set some foundations about the measurement of time and can move our discussion and examination to the purpose of this book, i.e. the last six days of Jesus life on earth.

It will be necessary at times to quote many of these writings again. We quoted them to explain the measurement of time. It will be necessary to repeat them to discuss various issues etc.

I thank you in advance for being understanding regarding the repeating of the passages.

Chapter 10

Passover or Last Supper

In reviewing my studies of twenty plus years, it is necessary for me to speak up about my opinion then. I can see a dramatic change in my writing from then and now. At that time I was a Christian Pastor who was Jewish. I did not practice Judaism. I knew little about Judaism. What I was learning was beginning to have an impact on me. I was being torn in pieces. It was difficult! It was challenging! It was horrible!! I was searching for an exit. I wanted to escape at times... I was beginning to feel the pressure of all the power and influence of my upbringing. At that time and at that place in my exploration, I was loosing perspective. I was beginning to squeeze information into places that suited my beliefs. My objectivity was being seriously challenged. Then, I was an ardent supporter of the beliefs many Christians hold dear, even when I knew they may not be accurate or even worse, entirely false. It was an awful place to be.

We will soon be approaching a subject in this book that I struggled to find an acceptable answer with. When I write, an acceptable answer, what I am trying to say is an answer that I could continue to believe the Christian Writings! I see many Christians doing what I did. I read in black and white what the Christian Writings said, but could not accept what I read. I felt like the problem was with me. If I believed more and stronger God would show me an answer out of this confusing position. Preparation Day was the crack in the floor or ceiling that I needed. In a little while, God Willing, we will begin a review of where Jesus is quoted by Matthew as saying,

Matthew 12:40
For as Jonas was three days and three nights in the whale's belly; so shall the Son of man be three days and three nights in the heart of the earth.

This verse presented a mountain high problem for me. At the time I wasn't ready to acknowledge the problems this verse presented to Christianity, so I searched and searched for an escape that would allow me to continue believing what I was taught. The escape that I am about to discuss is not justified. A few Christian scholars argue that when the Christian Writings uses the words Preparation Day it could mean the day leading up to Passover. It very well may. They argue that the Christian Writings's usage of the word Sabbath in Luke 23:54 was in reference to Passover since one is supposed to rest on Passover like one rests on the Sabbath. I accepted the case they were arguing because at that time and place in life the other side of the coin was unmentionable!

Luke 23:54
And that day was the preparation, and the Sabbath drew on.

I argued in favor of John's comments.

John 13: 1 – 5
Now before the Feast of the Passover [Seder Meal], when Jesus knew that his hour was come that he should depart out of this world unto the Father, having loved his own which were in the world, he loved them unto the end. And Supper

being ended, the devil having now put into the heart of Judas Iscariot, Simon's son, to betray him; Jesus knowing that the Father had given all things into his hands, and that he was come from God, and went to God; He rose from Supper, and laid aside his garments; and took a towel, and girded himself. After that he poured the water into a basin, he began to wash the disciples feet, and then to wipe them with the towel wherewith he was girded.

There is no question; John clearly stated that this Supper was before the Passover Seder Meal. This helps to support the argument Jesus died before the Passover Seder Meal. The concept that went along with this line of thought was because the Last Super was before the Passover Seder Meal we could push the chronological time of the Last Super to Wednesday night so this would better fit within Matthew 12:40's three days and three night.

For awhile I was open to this line of thought. However I eventually faced the facts as presented in the last chapter of this book. John's timing is incorrect.

Now having written this, we need to review what the other three Writers had to say about John's claim of this being the Last Super instead of the Passover Seder.

Matthew 26: 17 – 20
Matthew Wrote:
Now on the first day of the Feast of Unleavened Bread the disciples came to Jesus, saying to him, Where do you want us to prepare for you to eat the Passover [Seder Meal]? And he said, Go into the city to such a man, and say to him, The Master says, my time is at hand; I will keep the Passover [Seder Meal] at your house with my disciples. And the disciples did as Jesus had directed them; and they made ready the Passover [Seder Meal]. Now when the even was come, he sat down with the twelve. And as they did eat...'

Matthew says Jesus ate the Passover meal with his Disciples. John says it was a meal before the Passover Seder. John calls the meal a supper...

John does not reveal anything about who prepared the meal or where the meal was. Matthew gives some information. **Which account do you believe?**

This is where I was many years ago. My thought was to review Mark's account and Luke's account to see if I could support one of these positions. Let's do this...

Mark 14:12 – 18.
Mark Wrote:
And the first day of Unleavened Bread, when they killed the Passover [lamb], his disciples said to him, where do you want [us to go] that we may prepare that you may eat the Passover [Seder Meal]? And he sent forth two of his disciples, and said to them, you go into the city, and there you will meet a man bearing a pitcher of water follow him wherever he goes. Say to the Goodman of the house, The Master said, where is the guest chamber, where I shall eat the Passover [Seder Meal] with my disciples? And he will show you a large upper room furnished and prepared: there make ready for us. And his disciples went forth,

and came into the city, and found as he had said to them: and they made ready the Passover [Seder Meal]. And in the evening he came with the twelve. And as they sat and did eat...'

Mark's statement is more factual. Mark lets the reader know that the room is an upper room, which is furnished and prepared for the Passover Seder Meal. Mark's writings clearly state the question to the Goodman. *Where is the guest chamber, where I shall eat the Passover [Seder meal] with my disciples?* There is no mixing of words with Marks writing. Mark is speaking about the Passover Seder Meal.

The writers Matthew and Mark clearly state Jesus Observed the Passover Seder Meal. Their accounts do not agree with John's account that it was before Passover and that it was a supper. At this point I really wanted to examine Luke's account. What else was I to do? These three accounts in the Christian Writings clearly do not agree. What do you think? Which account is correct? **Back then I didn't know? I searched and searched! I questioned and questioned! I**

cried out to God what do I do?

Luke 22:7 – 14.
Luke Wrote:
Then came the day of Unleavened Bread, when the Passover [lamb] must be killed. And he sent Peter and John, saying, Go and prepare us the Passover [Seder Meal] that we may eat. And they said to him, where will you [have us go] that we [may] prepare? And he said to them, Behold, when you enter into the city, there a man will meet you, bearing a pitcher of water; follow him into the house where he enters in. And you shall say to the Goodman of the house, The Master says to you, Where is the guest chamber, where I shall eat the Passover [Seder Meal] with my disciples? And he will show you a large upper room furnished: there make ready. And they went, and found as he had said to them: and they made ready the Passover [Seder Meal]. And when the hour was come, he sat down, and the twelve apostles with him…'

Luke's accounting is quite troubling because he reveals that he knows the two disciples that

Jesus sent to prepare the Passover Seder Meal. It is especially troubling because the writer of John is one of the two disciples Jesus sent. John does not provide information as Mark and Luke do. John says it was before Passover. Mathew, Mark and Luke say Jesus ate the Passover Seder Meal. They say it was Passover. John says it was just a supper. Who is correct? John was there. It is possible that Matthew was also there. It is possible that Matthew was one of the twelve. This is the opinion of many Christian Scholars. We do not know. At the time, this was very difficult for me. Now it may be difficult for you as well... So what <u>are</u> you going to do with this information? I asked other knowledgeable people. They would just frown and often lower their head and say something like, *just believe.* I tried, I did that for a while but it didn't work for me. At that time I believed the Christian Writings were Divinely Inspired. I believed the Christian Writings were perfect. My world was shattered! My confidence was shaken. I spoke with my parents who were pastors for more than forty plus years. They could not provide any answers. My father criticized my education. He said,

George you are too educated! I hung in there for a while. I shared my concerns with my wife and close friends. No one had any answers. This was a difficult place to be. Reader, this may be where you are now. I don't know. At that time I chose what appeared to be the lesser of two problems. Later, I came to an acknowledgement that what I had believed and had been taught to believe all my life was inaccurate. Having a mother who was born Jewish but who did not live as a Jew, I turned to Judaism and to the Rabbis for answers. The answers were very slow in coming. I tossed and turned for years over these issues. I did not want to make a mistake. I did not want to deny the inspiration of the Christian Writings. I did not want to face what the writings in the Christian Writings said. It was horrible! It was awful! If you are there, I understand. I was taught from a young child up, that people who did not believe in Jesus would die and go to hell, a place of pain, of fire of torment forever for eternity. That was a very sobering thought for an Independent Fundamental Baptist Pastor standing at this crossroads of life.

You may end up at the crossroads just as I did. I don't know.

When we explore a possibility, there needs to be some proof something or some reference that could possibly substantiate a position! I found the possibility. I clung to the possibility of it being Preparation Day. This was not the truthful answer! It was a crutch for me. I knew better! This position did not hold water. I had to try something. For a short time I allowed myself to be confused. I saw the conflict between John and Matthew, Mark and Luke. It mattered very much yet it didn't matter because it was all over for me. I realized that the Christian Writings were not Divinely inspired and that the Christian Writings were not perfect. My exploration of The Last Six Days of Jesus Life on Earth came to a conclusion. I could not continue my study of this subject. I did not like the choices facing me. I wanted the choices to be different, but they were not. I did not write these four books. Yet, I had to deal with the shattered pieces they left behind.

Dear Reader, we are now going to begin a review

of what I term the three theories about Jesus death.

Theory One

If Jesus died late Wednesday...
n = night / d = day

Sat	Sun	Mon	Tue	Wed	Thu	Fri	Sat	Sun
				n1	n2	n3	n4	
					d1	d2	d3	

This scenario does allow for three days and for three nights if Jesus died late Wednesday. However the fact show Jesus died late Friday as we shall see.

Some scholars argue part nights and part days will work. I do not agree based upon the text. The text indicates it is three complete days and nights. Another issue is that Matthew quotes Jesus as saying *three days and three nights.* This is the reverse order of the Biblical measurement for time. I find this strange. Let's consider the part day part night theory.

Theory Two

If Jesus died late Thursday...
n = night / pn = partial night
d = day / pd = partial day

Sat	Sun	Mon	Tue	Wed	Thu	Fri	Sat	Sun
					n1	n2	pn3	
					pd1	d2	d3	

This theory does not agree with the requirement that the reference in Matthew 12:40 requires. Jesus must spend 3 - 24 hour periods in the grave, i.e. three entire days and three entre nights. If Jesus died on Thursday at the ninth hour, followers of this theory say this counts as one day. Friday would be day 2. Saturday would be day 3.

Let's consider just the nights. Thursday is night 1. Friday is night 2. However Saturday according to the Gospels is only a part night. However this theory accepts a part night. Why is night three a part night?

Matthew 28:1
In the end of the Sabbath, **as it began to dawn toward the first day of the week,** came Mary Magdalene and the other Mary to see the sepulcher.

Mark 16:1
And when the Sabbath was past, Mary Magdalene, and Mary the mother of James, and Salome, had bought sweet spices, that they might come and anoint him. **And very early in the morning the first day** of the week, they came unto the sepulcher **at the rising of the sun**.

Luke 24:1, 2
Now upon the first day of the week, **very early in the morning,** they came unto the sepulcher, bringing the spices which they had prepared, and certain others with them. And they found the stone rolled away from the sepulcher.

John 20.1
The first day of the week Mary Magdalene came early, when it was yet dark, unto the

sepulcher, and saw the stone taken away from the sepulcher.

We have varying accounts. Yet, several accounts say, it was still dark... at the end of Sabbath... So we see why there is a need to accept a partial night.

Theory Three

The third account ignores Matthew 12:40 entirely.

If Jesus died late Thursday...
n = night / pn = partial night
d = day / pd = partial day

Sat	Sun	Mon	Tue	Wed	Thu	Fri	Sat	Sun
						n1	pn2	
						pd2	d2	

What do you think? Does one of these theories work for you? Actually, as we shall see, none of these theories work. We see there is a real challenge trying to determine when Jesus died. Yet, we can figure this out. We have to re-review the information. If other clues are there, we must find them. I think one of the strong points is Luke identifies John as being one of the disciples who Jesus sent to prepare the Passover Seder Meal. John was there. John was an eye witness. We don't know about the other three. How did they gather their information. They do not share this with us. Yet, John was in his nineties when he wrote this Gospel of John. It is possible he may have had some memory issues. We don't know. On the other hand he may have intended to correct the record of Matthew, Mark and Luke. We don't know. He does not say. He could have clarified this for us but didn't. So we must look for other clues.

In Judaism the witness of two Jews could establish who is correct here. Yet, I cannot say with certainty that Mark and Luke were Jewish.

Are there any additional facts that could help us? Yes! Matthew, Mark and Luke each make reference to the fact that this was the First Day of Unleavened Bread.

Matthew Says,
Matthew 26:17
Now on the first day of the Feast of Unleavened Bread the disciples came to Jesus, saying to him, Where do you want us to prepare for you to eat the Passover [Seder Meal]?

Mark Says,
Mark 14:12
And the first day of Unleavened Bread, when they killed the Passover [lamb], his disciples said to him, where do you want [us to go] that we may prepare that you may eat the Passover [Seder Meal]?

Luke Says,
Luke 22:7
Then came the day of Unleavened Bread, when the Passover [lamb] must be killed. And he sent Peter and John, saying, Go and prepare us the Passover [Seder Meal] that we may eat.

The reference to the fact that 'his disciples came' in Matthew and Mark give the impression that his disciples, as a group of twelve men, came to him.

Regardless of how many came to Jesus, the fact remains that after these words were written, the disciples which remained could have disputed this. Only John disputes this. Peter says nothing. There was time for the disciples to speak up and say Matthew's account is wrong. We read of no other disciple supporting John's position that this was a supper instead of the Passover Seder Meal. This weighs heavy against John. In addition to this Mark and Luke make reference to this the day when the Passover lamb must be killed. Again, we read of only John disputing this. Luke informs us that it was Peter and John that made the preparations. Besides the disciples there were a number of individuals familiar with the details that could have supported either position but didn't. Based on this, I have to accept the witness of Matthew, Mark and Luke over John.

However, regardless of who is correct, the contradictions between the gospel writers are evident. From this we see the Christian Writings are NOT Divinely Inspired!! They have serious errors!

It is clear that from the Gospel writers that it is not possible to accurately say when Jesus died. Is there any more information that could be helpful? Yes. We return to Luke.

Luke 23:52 – 56
This man went unto Pilate, and begged the body of Jesus. And he took it down, and wrapped it in linen, and laid it in a sepulcher that was hewn in stone, wherein never man before was laid. And that day was the preparation, and the Sabbath drew on. And the women also, which came with him from Galilee, followed after, and beheld the sepulcher, and how his body was laid. And they returned, and prepared spices and ointments; and rested the Sabbath Day according to the Commandment.

There are several points. I have already shown that the Gospel writer clearly knew what Sabbath was, what the Preparation Day was, What The Day of Unleavened Bread was and what Passover was. Each writer has displayed the proper use of these terms. Review the examples I provided. It is clear that Luke's reference was to the Seventh Day of the week. The ladies prepared the burial spices Friday evening before the Seventh Day began. Then on the first day of the week they brought those spices to the tomb. In addition Luke says *they rested on the Sabbath Day according to the Commandment.*

This is clearly in reference to the Sabbath day. The Seventh Day is the only Day referred to as the Day of Rest. In addition to this, NO REFERENCE is made to the Passover Seder Meal. Why? If the Preparation Day was in reference to Passover instead of Sabbath Day, Luke would have noted that the ladies participated in the Passover Seder Meal and the recounting of the deliverance of Israel from Egypt. None of this was mentioned.

Exodus 31.15 – 17
Six days may work be done; but in the Seventh is the Sabbath of Rest, It is Holy to the Lord: Whosoever does any work in the Sabbath Day, he shall surely be put to death. Wherefore the Children of Israel shall keep the Sabbath, to Observe the Sabbath throughout their

generations, for a perpetual covenant. It is a sign between me and the Children of Israel for ever: for in six days the Lord Made heaven and earth, and on the Seventh Day He Rested, and was refreshed.

We are going to take about a 13 page detour where we will examine the chronology from the 8th of the month to the 12th of the month according to John.. The purpose in doing this is to examine the writer John's claim that Jesus only had a supper and that Jesus did not partake of the Passover Seder meal.

Chapter 11

Let The Detour Begin

BEGIN DETOUR

Dear Reader, we are going to piece together the Writer John's position of what happened. The evidence in this book shows that the Writer John's dates are wrong. Yet, the only way we will know this is to review his chronology. I call John's chronology a detour when in actuality it's more like getting lost. So for the sake of having a thorough discussion let's review the chronology if Jesus were buried on Wednesday. This would mean Tuesday evening Jesus and his disciples had their supper. This would have been the 12th Day of the First Month. Then all the events written from John 13:1 through 19:42 would have to take place between Tuesday night through Wednesday night. According to John, Wednesday was the Preparation day for Passover and Wednesday night was when the Passover Seder Meal began. INCORRECT!! Remember the Biblical day begins at night fall. This means Wednesday would have had to be the 14th Day of the first month. Yet, the facts do not support John's claims as we shall see. It would be almost 23 hours later that the Passover Lamb would be killed in the Temple Court Yard.

Returning to John's account, after dark the day would change to the 14th of the month. Reader, go back and look at theory 1. For Jesus to be a prophet and to fulfill his words in Matthew 12:40 he would have to be buried before dark on Wednesday. John's account tries to accomplish this...

John 19:16
When Pilate therefore heard that saying, he brought Jesus forth, and sat down in the judgment seat in a place that is called the Pavement, but in the Hebrew, Gabbatha. And it was the Preparation of the Passover, and about the Sixth hour: and he saith unto the Jews, Behold your King!

John 19:31
The Jews therefore, because it was the preparation, that the bodies should not remain

upon the cross on the Sabbath Day, (for that Sabbath Day was an High Day,) besought Pilate that their legs might be broken, and that they might be taken away.

John 19:41, 42
Now in the place where he was crucified there was a garden; and in the garden a new sepulcher, wherein was never man yet laid. There laid they Jesus therefore because of the Jews' preparation day; for the sepulcher was nigh at hand.

This means Wednesday night would be the Passover Seder Meal. Wednesday night would be Jesus' first night in the grave. It means late on Wednesday the men of Israel would be preparing to kill the Passover Lamb. This means that the celebration of the first day of Passover would end at dark on Thursday night. **I don't understand something.** Why didn't The ladies travel to the Tomb on Friday morning? There was nothing preventing them from traveling to the tomb of Jesus on Friday morning. The Weekly Sabbath would begin on Friday night at dark. Why would the ladies wait two additional days before bringing the spices? This does not make sense!

John 12:1
Then Jesus, six days before the Passover came to Bethany, where Lazarus was which had been dead, whom he raised from the dead. There they made him a supper; and Martha served: but Lazarus was one of them that sat at the table with him.

The key here is 6 days. If Passover began, this places Passover on Wednesday night instead of Thursday night. This is ONLY 5 day!

F	Sa	Su	M	T	W	Th	F	Sa	Su
8	9	10	11	12	13	14	15		
6	5	4	3	2	1	P			

The 8th Day of the First Month, Friday, late in the day Jesus came to Bethany.
This means Jesus came to Bethany during the day on Friday before Sabbath. This is correct.

Before we examine Matthew, Mark and Luke's accounting it is important to point out that they are unlike John's chronology. Matthew, Mark and Luke do not identify the day Jesus enters Bethany. If one were to place it on the 8th Day of the First Month everything in their accounting is a mess. We have a huge hole for several days in the middle of the week. This accounting goes in the face of what Christians teach about Jesus Triumphant Entry into Jerusalem. However if we begin with the First Day of the Week afterJesus death and work backwards as our chronology shows in the final chapter this places everyone on the same day for Jesus Triumphant Entry into Jerusalem. We deal with this later. When we place there chronological accounting in alignment with Sunday it works perfectly with the rest of the week for the most part. So even though I present their account of Jesus coming to Jerusalem here this is not where it belongs chronologically. This will soon be obvious. I CANNOT arbitrarily assign dates to the Writers of Matthew, Mark and Luke. However I do point out that they fit within a completely different chronology as stated. We must keep this in mind when reading the following accountings. John has Jesus coming to Bethany six days before Passover. Matthew, Mark and Luke do not begin their chronology until two days later on the 10th Day of the First Month, Sunday.

Matthew 21:1 – 17

This was on the 10th day of the month, Sunday.
And when they drew nigh unto Jerusalem, and were come to Bethphage, unto the mount of Olives, then sent Jesus two disciples, Saying unto them, Go into the village over against you, and straightway you shall find an ass tied, and a colt with her: loose them, and bring them unto me. And if any man say ought unto you, you shall say, The Lord hath need of them; and straightway he will send them. All this was done, that it might be fulfilled which was spoken by the prophet, saying, Tell you the daughter of Sion, Behold, thy King comes unto you, meek, and sitting upon an ass, and a colt the foal of an ass. And the disciples went, and did as Jesus commanded them, And brought the ass, and the colt, and put on them their clothes, and they set him thereon. And a very great multitude spread

their garments in the way; others cut down branches from the trees, and strawed them in the way. And the multitudes that went before, and that followed, cried, saying, Hosanna to the Son of David: Blessed is he that comes in the name of the Lord; Hosanna in the highest. And when he was come into Jerusalem, all the city was moved, saying, Who is this? And the multitude said, This is Jesus the prophet of Nazareth of Galilee. **And Jesus went into the Temple of God, and cast out all them that sold and bought in the Temple, and overthrew the tables of the moneychangers, and the seats of them that sold doves, And said unto them, It is written, My house shall be called the house of prayer; but ye have made it a den of thieves.** And the blind and the lame came to him in the Temple; and he healed them. And when the chief priests and scribes saw the wonderful things that he did, and the children crying in the Temple, and saying, Hosanna to the Son of David; they were sore displeased, And said unto him, Do you Hear what these are saying? And Jesus said to them, Yes; have you never read, Out of the mouth of babes and sucklings thou hast perfected praise? **And** *he left them, and went out of the city into Bethany; and he lodged there.* [The beginning of the 11th day]

Mark 11: 1 – 11
This was on the 10th day of the month, Sunday.

And when they came nigh to Jerusalem, unto Bethphage and Bethany, at the mount of Olives, he sent forth two of his disciples, And said unto them, Go your way into the village over against you: and as soon as you are entered into it, you shall find a colt tied, whereon never man sat; loose him, and bring him. And if any man say unto you, Why do ye this? say to him that the Lord hath need of him; and straightway he will send him hither. And they went their way, and found the colt tied by the door without in a place where two ways met; and they loose him. And certain of them that stood there said unto them, Why are you, loosing the colt? And they said unto them even as Jesus had commanded: and they let them go. And they brought the colt to Jesus, and cast their garments on him; and he sat upon him. And many spread their garments in the way: and others cut down branches off the trees, and strawed them in the way. And they that went before, and they that followed, cried, saying, Hosanna; Blessed is he that comes in the name of the Lord: Blessed be the kingdom of our father David, that comes in the name of the Lord: Hosanna in the highest. And Jesus entered into Jerusalem, and into the Temple: and when he had looked round about upon all things, **and now the eventide was come, he went out unto Bethany with the twelve.** [The beginning of the 11th day]

Luke 19:28 – 48

This was on the 10th day of the month, Sunday.

And when he had thus spoken, he went before, ascending up to Jerusalem. And it came to pass, when he was come nigh to Bethphage and Bethany, at the mount called the mount of Olives, he sent two of his disciples, Saying, Go both of you into the village over against you; in the which at your entering you shall find a colt tied, whereon yet never man sat: loose him, and bring him hither. *And if any man ask you, Why are you loosing him? thus shall you say unto him, Because the Lord hath need of him. And they* *that were sent went their way, and found even as he had said unto them. And as they were loosing the colt, the owners thereof said unto them, Why are you loosing the colt? And they said, The Lord hath need of him. And they brought him to Jesus: and they cast their garments upon the colt, and they set Jesus thereon. And as he went, they spread their clothes in the way. And when he was come nigh, even now at the descent of the mount of Olives, the whole multitude of the disciples began to rejoice and praise God with a loud voice for all the mighty works that they had seen; Saying, Blessed be the King that comes in the name of the Lord: peace in heaven, and glory in the highest. And some of the Pharisees from among the multitude said unto him, Master, rebuke thy disciples. And he answered and said unto them, I tell you that, if these should hold their peace, the stones would immediately cry out. And when he was come near, he beheld the city, and wept over it, Saying, If you had known, even thou, at least in this your day, the things which belong unto your peace! but now they are hid from thine eyes. For the days shall come upon thee, that thine enemies shall cast a trench about thee, and compass thee round, and keep thee in on every side, And shall lay thee even with the ground, and thy children within thee; and they shall not leave in thee one stone upon another; because you did not know the time of visitation.* **And he went into the Temple, and began to cast out them that sold therein, and them that bought; Saying unto them, It is written, My house is the house of prayer: but ye have made it a den of thieves.** *And he taught daily in the Temple...* [This was the 11th day of the month].

What we have just read is John's chronology beginning on the 8th Day of the First Month while Matthew, Mark and Luke's chronology begin on the 10th Day of the First Day of the Month. Notice that the verse says when the eventide was come Jesus *went out unto Bethany with the twelve. Jesus went to the house of Lazarus where he shared an Erev Shabbat meal as John described.*

The 9th Day of the Month [Sabbath]
That evening Jesus shared an Erev Sabbath meal with his friends. John makes this out to be a

big event.

John 12:2 – 5
This is on the 9th day of the month, Sabbath.

There they made him a supper; and Martha served: but Lazarus was one of them that sat at the table with him. Then took Mary a pound of ointment of spikenard, very costly, and anointed the feet of Jesus, and wiped his feet with her hair: and the house was filled with the odour of the ointment. Then saith one of his disciples, Judas Iscariot, Simon's son, which should betray him, Why was not this ointment sold for three hundred pence, and given to the poor?

Mark Says on the morrow, this would seem to be saying Sabbath. However when the eventide was come Jesus went out unto Bethany with the twelve. So like in John, 'On the morrow' would be referring to Sunday. The description of verses 12 – 19 does not fit Sabbath. Jesus did not curse the fig tree and cast money exchangers out of the Temple on Sabbath. Money exchangers would not be working on Sabbath at the Holy Temple.

Mark 11:12 – 19

This is the 11th day of the month, Monday.

And on the morrow, [Monday] when they were come from Bethany, he was hungry: And seeing a fig tree afar off having leaves, he came, if haply he might find any thing thereon: and when he came to it, he found nothing but leaves; for the time of figs was not yet. And Jesus answered and said unto it, No man eat fruit of thee hereafter for ever. And his disciples heard it. And they come to Jerusalem: and **Jesus went into the Temple, and began to cast out them that sold and bought in the Temple, and overthrew the tables of the moneychangers, and the seats of them that sold doves; And would not suffer that any man should carry any vessel through the temple.** *And he taught, saying unto them, Is it not written, My house shall be called of all nations the house of prayer? but ye have made it a den of thieves. And the scribes and chief priests heard it, and sought how they might destroy him: for they feared him, because all the people was astonished at his doctrine.* **And when even was come, he went out of the city.** [This is the 12th day of the month]

John 12:12 – 15

This is the 10th Day of the month, Sunday.

On the next day much people that were come to the feast, when they heard that Jesus was coming to Jerusalem, Took branches of palm trees, and went forth to meet him, and cried, Hosanna: Blessed is the King of Israel that cometh in the name of the Lord. And Jesus, when he had found a young ass, sat thereon; as it is written, Fear not, daughter of Sion: behold, thy King cometh, sitting on an ass's colt.

On the next day- This is a difficult passage. Why? One has to determine if John is making reference to 'in the morning' which was Sabbath Morning or if John was making reference to the Sunday. One can argue either way. We are going to go with the next day to mean Sunday, 4 days before Passover. Why? It is not likely that Jews would break or cut palm tree branches on Sabbath. Luke says this is the day Jesus cast out money exchangers.

Dear Reader all four Gospel writers have Jesus coming to Jerusalem on the 8th day of the month.

Matthew, Mark and Luke have Jesus entering the Temple on Friday. This was Jesus first entry. John has Jesus entering the Holy City on Sunday.

END DETOUR

Chapter 12

More Conflict With John

Mark 11:20, 27; 13.1
This is the 11th Day of the Month, Monday.
And in the morning, as they passed by, they saw the fig tree dried up from the roots.. And they come again to Jerusalem: and as he was walking in the Temple... And as he went out of the temple, one of his disciples saith unto him, Master, see what manner of stones and what buildings are here?

John's next entry is on Tuesday night which is the beginning of the 13th Day of the month.
John 13:1 – 19:42

This is the 13th Day of the Month which begins Tuesday night what many term the Last Supper. From this point through Wednesday according to John Jesus was tried and killed.

Matthew 26:2
This is the 12th Day of the Month, Tuesday.

Do you know that after two days is the Feast of the Passover [Seder Meal], and the Son of man is betrayed to be crucified?

Mark 14:1
This is the 12th Day of the Month, Tuesday.
After two days was the Feast of the Passover, and of Unleavened Bread: and the chief priests and the scribes sought how they might take him by craft, and put him to death.

Now we have another very serious conflict with the writer John. Matthew is quoting Jesus as saying in two days is the Festival of Passover when the son of man will be betrayed and crucified. Yet according to John that very night would be Jesus final supper. And the next day Jesus would be killed and placed in a tomb. So who do you believe Jesus or John?

The writer Mark reinforces Matthew. It is two days until the Passover Seder Meal.

The story in Matthew 26:6 -15 appears to be the same story the writer John gave in John 12:2 - 8.

John places the story of the precious ointment as having taken place on Erev Shabbat at Lazarus home. Matthew places the story on the 13th Day of the First Month at Simon the leper's home. The stories are two different stories.

Luke 22:7
The 14th Day of Passover, Thursday.
Then came the day of unleavened bread, when the Passover [Lamb] must be killed. And [Jesus] sent Peter and John, saying, Go and prepare us the passover, that we may eat.

That evening we see Jesus sitting down with his disciples to eat the Passover Seder Meal.

Mathew 26.20, 21
Now when the even was come, he sat down with the twelve. And as they did eat, he said, Verily I say unto you, that one of you shall betray me.

Mark 14:17, 18
And in the evening he cometh with the twelve. And as they sat and did eat, Jesus said, Verily I say unto you, One of you which eats with me

shall betray me.

Luke 22:13 – 15
And they went, and found as he had said unto them: and they made ready the Passover [Seder Meal]. And when the hour was come, he sat down, and the twelve apostles with him. And he said unto them, With desire I have desired to eat this Passover [Seder Meal] with you before I suffer:

Dear Ones as we conclude this chapter I have provided many references including to quotes from Jesus that conflicted with the writer Johns recollection. Matthew quotes Jesus as saying in 'two days is the Festival of Passover when the son of man will be betrayed and crucified. Luke quotes Jesus as saying, *'With desire I have desired to eat this Passover [Seder Meal] with you before I suffer:'*

We each must draw a conclusion of some kind. I concluded that there are a number of conflicting statements in the four Gospels. There are scholars that support one of three theories regarding when Jesus died and allegedly arose. Each theory is wrong. Among the Gospel Writers, three of the writers support that Jesus died on Friday. This ruins the first theory of three 24 hour days and nights in the grave are voided. The second theory of partial days is very weak. Matthew 12:40 clearly says as or like Jonah was three days and three nights does not allow for partial days or partial nights. Then the third theory which ignores Matthew 12:40 is lack seriousness. It is openly impossible.

It is clear to me that Jesus did not rise from the dead so the theories mean nothing in the first place. It is clear to me that Jesus is a false prophet. Matthew 12: 40 was not fulfilled. Then there is the debate over the Preparation Day. It is clear except where stated that the Preparation Day is in regards to Sabbath. The writer John's position is not well supported!

I did not come to this position immediately years ago. Arriving here requires much study.

Chapter 13

So What Really Happened?

The calendar below will guide us chronologically through the last days of Jesus' life on earth.

Column one shows the Hebrew day of the week by number.

Column two shows the names of the days according to the Gregorian Calendar.

Column three shows the numbers 8 through 17 with each representing the number for that specific Hebrew Calendar Day for the first month.

Column four shows the number of days to P = Passover. This is a count down to Passover which begins with John 12.1

6	7	1	2	3	4	5	6	7	1
F	S	S	M	T	W	T	F	S	S
8	9	10	11	12	13	14	15	16	17
6	5	4	3	2	1	P			

Passover Calendar for the First Month in the Year Jesus died

Hebrew Days of the Week for the 1st Month						
1	2	3	4	5	6	7
					1	2
3	4	5	6	7	8	9
10	11	12	13	14	15	16
17	18	19	20	21	22	23
24	25	26	27	28	29	30

Hebrew Calendar with Gregorian Week Days						
S	M	T	W	T	F	S
					1	2
3	4	5	6	7	8	9
10	11	12	13	14	15	16
17	18	19	20	21	22	23
24	25	26	27	28	29	30

Index of Days For First Month

Day	Page
8th Day of the First Month - Friday	160
9th Day of the First Month / Fri. Night	160
9th Day of the First Month - Saturday	-
10th Day of the First Month - Sunday	161
11th Day of the First Month - Monday	166
12th Day of the First Month / Mon. Night	168
12th Day of the First Month - Tuesday	170
13th Day of the First Month / Tue. Night	173
13th Day of the First Month – Wed.	174
14th Day of the First Month / Wed. Night	174
14th Day of the First Month - Thursday	174
15th Day of the First Month / Thur. Night	177
15th Day of the First Month - Friday	180
16th Day of the First Month - Sabbath	-
17th Day of the First Month - Sunday	185

Friday
The 8th Day of the First Month
Jesus came to Bethany on Friday the 8th Day of the First Month. This was at the end of the 8th Day. John says, Six Days 'BEFORE' Passover. This means there were six full days until Passover.

Friday Night
The 9th Day of the First Month
That even was Erev Sabbath. Jesus enjoyed his last Erev Sabbath meal with friends in Bethany. That night John writes that Mary anointed Jesus feet and wiped them dry with her hair. This type of action is entirely out of bounds with regards to how Observant men and women interact with each other. Paul warns about touching.

1 Corinthians 7:1
Now concerning the things whereof you wrote unto me: **It is good for a man not to touch a woman.**

The logic behind this is a man does not know when a woman is unclean from her time of the month. Just the same, a woman should not instigate touching a man other than her husband, father and her sons etc. So what I am saying is the behavior in John 12:3 – 7 is quite strange especially for an Observant Rabbi.

Friday at nightfall was the 9th Day of the First Month.

John 12:1
Then Jesus six days before the Passover came to Bethany, where Lazarus was which had been dead, whom he raised from the dead. There they made him a supper; and Martha served: but Lazarus was one of them that sat at the table with him.

Sunday
The 10th Day of the First Month
Exodus 12.3 - 10
You, Speak unto all the congregation of Israel, saying, In the tenth day of this month they shall take to them every man a lamb, according to the house of their fathers, a lamb for an house: And if the household be too little for the lamb, let him

and his neighbor next unto his house take it according to the number of the souls; every man according to his eating shall make your count for the lamb. Your lamb shall be without blemish, a male of the first year: you shall take it out from the sheep, or from the goats: And you shall keep it up until the fourteenth day of the same month: and the whole assembly of the congregation of Israel shall kill it in the evening. And they shall take of the blood, and strike it on the two side posts and on the upper door post of the houses, wherein they shall eat it. And they shall eat the flesh in that night, roast with fire, and unleavened bread; and with bitter herbs they shall eat it. Eat not of it raw, nor sodden at all with water, but roast with fire; his head with his legs, and with the purtenance thereof. And you shall let nothing of it remain until the morning; and that which remains of it until the morning you shall burn with fire.

When the Children of Israel were in Egypt the tenth of the First Month fell on Sabbath.

John 12.12 – 15

On the next day much people that were come to the feast, when they heard that Jesus was coming to Jerusalem, Took branches of palm trees, and went forth to meet him, and cried, Hosanna: Blessed is the King of Israel that cometh in the name of the Lord. And Jesus, when he had found a young ass, sat thereon; as it is written, Fear not, daughter of Sion: behold, thy King cometh, sitting on an ass's colt.

We have already discussed the term **'the next day'**. Still we MUST remember the evening in which Jesus enjoyed the supper together with his friends was the 9th Day of the First Month. The day that followed would be the next day. In addition based upon the Observances our Creator requires of the Children of Israel the events in John 12:12 - 15 could not have taken place on the Holy Sabbath. Therefore the next day had to be the 10th Day of the First Month. Jews are prohibited from buying and selling on Sabbath as described in Matthew 21:12; Luke 19:45. The 10th Day of the First Month was Sunday. This fits with the traditional Christian position that Jesus entered the Holy City of

Jerusalem as described in John 12:12 – 15. Christians call this day Jesus triumphant Entry into Jerusalem. In addition It is on this day the Children of Israel took a young lamb or goat and marched it through the streets in Egypt.

In the writings of Matthew, Mark and Luke each writer picks up their narrative with this day. Some Christian scholars argue that Jesus made two triumphant entries into Jerusalem based upon the difference in wording between the four Gospels. John (John 12:1) says Jesus went to Bethany. Matthew says, (Matthew 21:1) Jesus went to Bethphage then to the Mount of Olives. Mark says, (Mark 11:1) Jesus went to Bethphage, then to the Mount of Olives and then to Bethany. Luke says, (Luke 19:28, 29) Bethphage, then to the Mount of Olives and then to Bethany. I note these differences. Over the next few pages we will see if there is room to argue in favor of Jesus making two triumphant entries into Jerusalem. There is no room for Jesus to die on Wednesday the 13th Day of the First Month.

Matthew 21:12
And Jesus went into the temple of God, and cast out all them that sold and bought in the temple, and overthrew the tables of the moneychangers, and the seats of them that sold doves, 13 And said unto them, It is written, My house shall be called the house of prayer; but ye have made it a den of thieves.

Luke 19:45
And he went into the temple, and began to cast out them that sold therein, and them that bought; 46 Saying unto them, It is written, My house is the house of prayer: but ye have made it a den of thieves.

Sunday Night
The 11th Day of the First Month
After Jesus triumphant Entry into Jerusalem Matthew and Mark note that Jesus spent the entire day in the Temple then departed after evening prayers he went to Bethany. Night fall brings on the 11th Day of the First Month, Monday.

Matthew 21: 17
And he left them, and went out of the city into Bethany; and he lodged there.

Mark 11:11
And Jesus entered into Jerusalem, and into the temple: and when he had looked round about upon all things, and now the eventide was come, he went out unto Bethany with the twelve.

Now we note an important difference in the writings styles of Matthew and Mark. Matthew ties that night with the morning by saying, 'Now in the morning...' Mark also ties that that night with the morning by writing, 'And on the morrow...'.

Monday
The 11th Day of the First Month
Matthew 21:18 - 23
Now in the morning as he returned into the city, [of Jerusalem] he hungered. And when he saw a fig tree in the way, he came to it, and found nothing thereon, but leaves only, and said unto it, 'Let no fruit grow on thee henceforward for ever. And presently the fig tree withered away.' And

when the disciples saw it, they marveled, saying, 'How soon is the fig tree withered away!' Jesus answered and said unto them, 'Verily I say unto you, If you have faith, and doubt not, you shall not only do this which is done to the fig tree, but also if you shall say unto this mountain, Be thou removed, and be thou cast into the sea; it shall be done. And all things, whatsoever ye shall ask in prayer, believing, ye shall receive. **And when he was come into the Temple,** *the chief priests and the elders of the people came unto him as he was teaching, and said, By what authority doest thou these things***? and who gave thee this authority?**

Mark 11:12 – 17
And on the morrow, when they were come from Bethany, he was hungry: *And seeing a fig tree afar off having leaves, he came, if haply he might find any thing thereon: and when he came to it, he found nothing but leaves; for the time of figs was not yet. And Jesus answered and said unto it, 'No man eat fruit of thee hereafter for ever. And his disciples heard it.'* ***And they came to Jerusalem: and Jesus went into the Temple,*** *and*

began to cast out them that sold and bought in the temple, and overthrew the tables of the moneychangers, and the seats of them that sold doves; And would not suffer that any man should carry any vessel through the Temple. And he taught, saying unto them, 'Is it not written, My house shall be called of all nations the house of prayer? but ye have made it a den of thieves.'

Monday Night
The 12th Day of the First Month
The events from Matthew 21:18 through Matthew 24:1 happen on Monday, the 11th Day of the First Month. Later Jesus exits the Temple for awhile. His Disciples follow him with more questions. Again, Jesus spends Monday at the Temple Teaching then departs again after evening prayers. Night fall brings on the 12th Day of the First Month.

Matthew 24:1- 3
And Jesus went out, and departed from the Temple: and his disciples came to him for to shew him the buildings of the Temple. And Jesus said unto them, See you not all these things?

verily I say unto you, 'There shall not be left here one stone upon another, that shall not be thrown down.' And as he sat upon the Mount of Olives, the disciples came unto him privately, saying, 'Tell us, when shall these things be? and what shall be the sign of thy coming, and of the end of the world?'

The discussion continued from Matthew 24:1 through until Matthew 26:2. It was toward evening.

Matthew 26:1, 2
And it came to pass, when Jesus had finished all these sayings, he said unto his disciples, 'Do you know that after two days is the Feast of the Passover, and the Son of man is betrayed to be crucified?'

It is important to note that it is 'after two days' NOT in two days. After two days means after Tuesday and After Wednesday the next day, Thursday was the Passover. This is correct. At night fall on Thursday the Passover began.

Mark 11:19
And when even was come, he went out of the city.

Dear Reader it is here at this point that John 13 kicks back in so to speak. I should say if one believed John's writings more than Matthew, Mark and Luke's writings then it is here on Tuesday Night that Jesus has his final supper. We have already discussed the issues with John's accounting. We continue. As mention earlier night fall brings on the 12th Day of the First Month, Tuesday. Mark ties the night with the following morning.

Tuesday
The 12th Day of the First Month
Mark 11:20
And in the morning, as they passed by, they saw the fig tree dried up from the roots. And Peter calling to remembrance said unto him, 'Master, behold, the fig tree which you cursed is withered away.' And Jesus answering said unto them, 'Have faith in God. For verily I say unto you, That whosoever shall say unto this mountain, Be thou

removed, and be thou cast into the sea; and shall not doubt in his heart, but shall believe that those things which he says shall come to pass; he shall have whatsoever he saith. Therefore I say unto you, What things soever you desire, when ye pray, believe that you receive them, and you shall have them. And when you stand praying, forgive, if you have ought against any: that your Father also which is in heaven may forgive you your trespasses. But if ye do not forgive, neither will your Father which is in heaven forgive your trespasses.' **And they come again to Jerusalem: and as he was walking in the Temple,** *there come to him the chief priests, and the scribes, and the elders, And say unto him, 'By what authority do you do these things?'*

After Jesus spent Tuesday in the Temple teaching he went out that afternoon. Again the disciples came to him. Now the discussion in Matthew 24:1 – 26:2 and the discussion in Mark 13:1 - 37 are similar. Is it possible that either Matthew or Mark got it wrong? Yes! Is it possible Matthew missed a day? Yes, it is likely. Yet, it really does not change anything. The discussion appears to be a bit different.

Mark 13:1-4
And as he went out of the Temple, one of his disciples said unto him, 'Master, see what manner of stones and what buildings are here! And Jesus answering said unto him, Do you see these great buildings? There shall not be left one stone upon another, that shall not be thrown down. And as he sat upon the mount of Olives over against the Temple, Peter and James and John and Andrew asked him privately, Tell us, when shall these things be? And what shall be the sign when all these things shall be fulfilled?

Mark 14:1
After two days was the Feast of the Passover, and of Unleavened Bread: and the chief priests and the scribes sought how they might take him by craft, and put him to death.

Matthew writes, 'after two days IS the Feast of the Passover...' Mark writes about one day later, 'After two days WAS the Feast of the Passover, and of Unleavened Bread:' This is also correct.

After Wednesday and After Thursday is the Festival Passover Meal, i.e. The Festival of Unleavened Bread which happens at night fall. The WAS reflects on the past tense of the Passover on the 14th. After two days it will be past. So I fail to see the conflict. Nightfall ushers in the 13th Day of the First Month, Wednesday. Even though it is now night fall and a new day has begun, it is still Tuesday night by the Gregorian Calendar. It is on this night that Mark writes Jesus was in Bethany enjoying a meal with Simon the leper when a woman poured alabaster ointment on Jesus head.

Tuesday Night
The 13th Day of the First Month
Mark 14:3
And being in Bethany in the house of Simon the leper, as he sat at meat, there came a woman having an alabaster box of ointment of spikenard very precious; and she brake the box, and poured it on his head.

The only accounting of Jesus whereabouts are provided by Luke.

Wednesday
The 13th Day of the First Month
Luke 21:37, 38
And in the day time he was teaching in the Temple; and at night he went out, and abode in the mount that is called the mount of Olives. And all the people came early in the morning to him in the temple, for to hear him.

Wednesday Night
The 14th Day of the First Month
This is the only chronological accounting of what Jesus did on Wednesday or Wednesday night. At night fall the 14th Day of the First Month is ushered in. Matthew, Mark and Luke each pick up with Thursday the 14th Day of the First Month.

Thursday
The 14th Day of the First Month
Matthew 26:17 – 19
Now the First Day of the Feast of Unleavened Bread the disciples came to Jesus, inquiring from him, 'Where do you want us to prepare for you to eat the Passover [Seder Meal]? And he said, Go into the city to such a man, and say unto him,

The Master says, My time is at hand; I will keep the Passover [Seder Meal] at your house with my disciples. And the disciples did as Jesus had appointed them; and they made ready the Passover [Seder Meal].

Mark 14:12 – 16
And the First Day of Unleavened Bread, when they killed the Passover [lamb], his disciples said asked him, 'Where do you want us to go and prepare for you to eat the Passover [Seder Meal?' And he sent forth two of his disciples, and said unto them, ' You go into the city, and there you shall meet a man bearing a pitcher of water: follow him. And wheresoever he shall go in, you should say to the goodman of the house, The Master says, 'Where is the guestchamber, where I shall eat the Passover [Seder Meal] with my disciples?' And he will shew you a large upper room furnished and prepared: there make ready for us. And his disciples went forth, and came into the city, and found as he had said unto them: and they made ready the Passover [Seder Meal].

Luke 22:7 – 13

Then came the Day of Unleavened Bread, when the Passover [lamb] must be killed. And he sent Peter and John, saying, 'Go and prepare us the Passover [Seder Meal], that we may eat.' And they said unto him, 'Where do you want us to go prepare?' And he said unto them, 'Behold, when you have entered into the city, there a man will meet you, bearing a pitcher of water; follow him into the house where he enters in. And you shall say unto the goodman of the house, The Master says unto you, Where is the guestchamber, where I shall eat the Passover [Seder Meal] with my disciples? And he shall show you a large upper room furnished: there make ready. And they went, and found as he had said unto them: and they made ready the Passover Seder Meal.

The writings of Matthew, Mark and Luke simply do not agree with John. They speak for themselves. In each account Jesus sends his disciples into the Holy City to prepare the Passover Seder Meal. Peter and John kill the Passover lamb then prepare it. This was late in the afternoon of the 14th day of the First Month.

As mentioned before it is amazing that John would not recall this. Yet, Jesus enjoyed many meals that week.

The Passover Seder Meal
The Feast of Unleavened Bread
Thursday Night
The 15th Day of the First Month

At nightfall after evening prayers Jesus came to the upper room to eat the Passover Seder Meal, not the supper. The writer Luke makes it very clear that Jesus was eating the Passover Seder Meal. This was Thursday the 15th of the First Month.

Matthew 26:20, 21
Now when the even was come, he sat down with the twelve. And as they did eat, he said, Verily I say unto you, that one of you shall betray me.

Mark 14:17, 18
And in the evening he came with the twelve. And as they sat and did eat, Jesus said, Verily I say unto you, One of you which eats with me shall betray me.

Luke 22:7
And when the hour was come, he sat down, and the twelve apostles with him. And he said unto them, With desire I have desired to eat this Passover [Seder Meal] with you before I suffer: For I say unto you, I will not any more eat thereof, until it be fulfilled in the kingdom of God.

From this point on the chronology becomes an hour by hour chronology. So what I have chosen to do is to give a brief summary of the last day. The events of the last day are very important. However in the context of our examination of days we will conclude by showing Jesus died late Friday afternoon and that friends came on the first day of the week. We will pick this subject up in a third book, God Willing.

After the Passover Seder Meal Jesus goes to Gethsemane to pray. Judas brings a band of people and soldiers to apprehend Jesus. According to Matthew Jesus is arrested and taken to the Kohen Gadol / the High Priest where he is found guilty of blaspheming. He is then taken to Pontius Pilate, the governor to be questioned. According to Luke's writing when Pilate learns Jesus is a Galilean he sent Jesus to Herod where he was questioned and returned to Pilate. At that time of the year it was the custom of the governor to release a prisoner to the people. Pontius Pilate offers the crowd Jesus or Barabbas. The crowd selects Barabbas and cries out to crucify Jesus. Pilate tries to reason with the crowd but realizes it was useless. So he washes his hands to symbolize Jesus death would not be on him. Jesus is mocked and beaten by soldiers. A crown of thorns is placed on his head. He is spit upon. Then he is led to the place called skull. His cross is too heavy to bear so a man called Cyrene Simon is recruited to carry his cross. When they arrive at Golgotha Jesus is placed on the cross and crucified. He was crucified between two malefactors. A vast darkness covers the earth and in the late afternoon Jesus dies. Joseph asks Pilate to give him Jesus' body. Pilate agrees. Joseph with some help from Nicodemus wrap Jesus body and placed him in a tomb before the Sabbath began.

Passover Day
Friday
The 15th Day of the First Month
Matthew 27:46 - 50
And about the ninth hour Jesus cried with a loud voice, saying, Eli, Eli, lama sabachthani? that is to say, My God, my God, why hast thou forsaken me? Some of them that stood there, when they heard that, said, This man calleth for Elias. And straightway one of them ran, and took a sponge, and filled it with vinegar, and put it on a reed, and gave him to drink. The rest said, Let be, let us see whether Elias will come to save him. *Jesus, when he had cried again with a loud voice, yielded up the ghost.*

It is during the ninth hour that Jesus dies.

Mark 15:34 - 37
And at the ninth hour Jesus cried with a loud voice, saying, Eloi, Eloi, lama sabachthani? which is, being interpreted, My God, my God, why hast thou forsaken me? And some of them that stood by, when they heard it, said, Behold, he calleth Elias. And one ran and filled a sponge

full of vinegar, and put it on a reed, and gave him to drink, saying, Let alone; let us see whether Elias will come to take him down. **And Jesus cried with a loud voice, and gave up the ghost.**

Luke 23:44 - 46
And it was about the sixth hour, and there was a darkness over all the earth until the ninth hour. And the sun was darkened, and the veil of the temple was rent in the midst. **And when Jesus had cried with a loud voice, he said, Father, into thy hands I commend my spirit: and having said thus, he gave up the ghost.**

John 19:30
When Jesus therefore had received the vinegar, he said, It is finished: and he bowed his head, and gave up the ghost.

Jesus dies on Friday, Preparation Day for Sabbath, the 15th Day of the First Month.

Matthew 27:50 - 62
Jesus, when he had cried again with a loud voice, yielded up the ghost. *And, behold, the veil*

of the temple was rent in twain from the top to the bottom; and the earth did quake, and the rocks rent; And the graves were opened; and many bodies of the saints which slept arose, And came out of the graves after his resurrection, and went into the holy city, and appeared unto many. Now when the centurion, and they that were with him, watching Jesus, saw the earthquake, and those things that were done, they feared greatly, saying, Truly this was the Son of God. And many women were there beholding afar off, which followed Jesus from Galilee, ministering unto him: Among which was Mary Magdalene, and Mary the mother of James and Joses, and the mother of Zebedee's children. When the even was come, there came a rich man of Arimathaea, named Joseph, who also himself was Jesus 'disciple: He went to Pilate, and begged the body of Jesus. Then Pilate commanded the body to be delivered. And when Joseph had taken the body, he wrapped it in a clean linen cloth, And laid it in his own new tomb, which he had hewn out in the rock: and he rolled a great stone to the door of the sepulcher, and departed. And there was Mary Magdalene, and the other Mary, sitting over against the sepulcher.

Now the next day, that followed the day of the preparation, the chief priests and Pharisees came together unto Pilate,

Mark 15:37 - 41

And Jesus cried with a loud voice, and gave up the ghost. And the veil of the temple was rent in twain from the top to the bottom. And when the centurion, which stood over against him, saw that he so cried out, and gave up the ghost, he said, Truly this man was the Son of God. There were also women looking on afar off: among whom was Mary Magdalene, and Mary the mother of James the less and of Joses, and Salome; (Who also, when he was in Galilee, followed him, and ministered unto him;) and many other women which came up with him unto Jerusalem.

And now when the even was come, because it was the preparation, that is, the day before the sabbath, Joseph of Arimathaea, an honourable counsellor, which also waited for the kingdom of God, came, and went in boldly unto Pilate, and

craved the body of Jesus. *And Pilate marveled if he were already dead: and calling unto him the centurion, he asked him whether he had been any while dead. And when he knew it of the centurion, he gave the body to Joseph. And he bought fine linen, and took him down, and wrapped him in the linen, and laid him in a sepulcher which was hewn out of a rock, and rolled a stone unto the door of the sepulcher. And Mary Magdalene and Mary the mother of Joses beheld where he was laid.*

Luke 23:46 - 56
And when Jesus had cried with a loud voice, he said, Father, into thy hands I commend my spirit: and having said thus, he gave up the ghost. Now when the centurion saw what was done, he glorified God, saying, Certainly this was a righteous man. And all the people that came together to that sight, beholding the things which were done, smote their breasts, and returned. And all his acquaintance, and the women that followed him from Galilee, stood afar off, beholding these things.

And, behold, there was a man named Joseph, a counsellor; and he was a good man, and a just: (The same had not consented to the counsel and deed of them;) he was of Arimathaea, a city of the Jews: who also himself waited for the kingdom of God. This man went unto Pilate, and begged the body of Jesus. And he took it down, and wrapped it in linen, and laid it in a sepulcher that was hewn in stone, wherein never man before was laid. And that day was the preparation, and the sabbath drew on. And the women also, which came with him from Galilee, followed after, and beheld the sepulcher, and how his body was laid. And they returned, and prepared spices and ointments; and rested the Sabbath Day according to the Commandment.

Sunday
The 17th Day of the First Month
On the first day of the week all four writers describe visitors to Jesus tomb... This covers the Chronology of Jesus last six days on earth. Christians claim Jesus rose from the dead. I don't agree.

In another book entitled Passover, Jesus Last Hours we review the last hours of Jesus life on earth along with some critical points that dispute the resurrection allegations...

So we have come to the end of this book, PASSOVER - Jesus Last Six Days On Earth. Yet we have not reached the completion point. The points made in this book and the facts established will continue on. What I learned changed my life forever. What you have learned is up to you to decide what to do with.

References for Hebrew Scriptures

Exodus	
Ref.	Page
12.1	55
12:1, 2	59
12,3-10	161
12:14, 15	95
12:16, 17	96
12:18 – 20	96
13:4-5	58, 59
20:10, 11	86
20.12	25
31,15 – 17	132

Genesis	
1.5	61
1.8	61
1.13	61
1.14	53
1.19	61

1.23	61
1.31	62
2:2, 3	86
Numbers	
28.16,17	99
Psalms	
24	64
48	64
81	64
82	64
94.1 - 95.3	64
92	65
93	65

References for Christian Writings		
John	
1:39	46
2:13	46
2:23	46
4:6	46
5:9	46, 89
5:10	89
5:16	89
5:18	89
6:4	46
7:2	46
7:22	89
7:23	89
9:14	89
9:16	89
10:22	46
11:55	46
12:1	46, 138, 157, 161, 164

12:2-5	146
12:2-8	152
12:3-7	161
12:12-15	148, 162, 163, 164
13:1	46
13:1-5	115
13:1 -19:42	135, 151
18:28	46
19:14	46, 81
19:16	126, 136
19:27	46
19:30	83, 181
19:30-20:1	91
19:31	89, 108, 136
19:41	137
19:42	109, 137
20:1	62, 126

	Luke
1:59	45
2:41	45
2:44	45
4:16	45, 89
4:31	89
6:1	89
6.2	89
6.5	89
6.6	89
6.7	89
6.9	89
9:22	45
12:39	46
13:10	89
13:14	89
13:15	89
13:16	45, 89
14:1	45, 89

14:3	89
14:5	89
19:28, 29	164
19:45	163, 165
19:28-48	143
22:1	46 102
21:37, 38	174
22:7	46, 102, 120, 129, 153, 175, 178
22:8	46, 102, 120, 175
22:9	102, 120, 120, 175
22:10	102, 120, 175
22:11	46, 102, 120, 175
22:12	102, 120, 175
22:13	102, 120, 154, 175
22:14	46, 102, 120, 154
22:15	102, 154
22:16	102
22:17	102
23:43	46

23:44	46, 81, 83
23:44-46	83, 181
23:46-56	184
23:50-24:1	90
23:52	108, 131
23:53	108, 131
23:54	89, 108, 115, 131
23:55	46, 131
23:56	46, 131
24:1	46, 126
24:2	126
24:33	46
Mark	
1:21	45, 89
2:23	45, 89
2:24	89
2:27	89
2:28	89

6:2	45
9:31	45
10:34	45
11:1	164
11:1-11	142, 166
11:12-19	147, 167, 170
11:20	151, 170
11:27	151
12:12	45
13:1	151
13:1-4	172
13:1-37	171
13:35	46
14:1	45, 100, 152, 172
14:3	173
14:12	45, 100, 101, 118, 129, 175
14:13	101, 118, 175
14:14	45, 101, 118, 175
14:15	101, 118, 175

14:16	45, 101, 118, 175
14:17	101, 118, 153, 175, 177
14:18	118, 153, 177
14:37	46
14:41	46
15:25	46, 80
15:33	46, 81
15:34	46, 83
15:35	46, 83
15:34-37	83, 180
15:37-41	183
15:42	89, 107
15:52	45
16:1	89, 90, 126
16:2	45, 90
Matthew	
4:12	45
8:13	46

9:22	46
10:19	46
12:1	45. 80
12:2	89
12:5	89
12:8	89
12:10	89
12:11	89
12:12	89
12:40	45, 114, 127, 136, 155
13:1	45
15:28	46
15:32	45
16:21	45
17:1	45
17:18	46
17:23	45
20:2	46
20:5	46

20:6	46
20:12	46, 163
20:19	45
21:1	164
21:12	165
21:17	166
21:1-17	140
21:18	63, 168
21:18-23	166
22:23	45
24:1-3	168, 169
24:1 -26:2	171
24:20	
24:36	46
24:44	46
26:1	169
26:2	45, 151, 169
26:5	45
26:6-15	152

26:17	45, 67, 129, 174
26:18	67, 174
26:19	174
26:20, 21	153, 177
26:55	46
26:61	45
26:17	100, 117
26:18	100, 117
26:19	100, 117
26:20	100, 117
27:19	45
27:40	45
27:45	46, 81
27:46	46
27:46-50	82, 180
27:50-62	181, 182, 183
27:59	107
27:60	107
27:61	107

27:62	45, 107
27:64	45
28:1	45, 89, 126

1 Corinthians	
7:1	160

About The Author

Dr. Akiva Gamliel Belk

Jewish, Husband, Father, Grandfather and Step Great Grandfather.

Graduate:
A.A. Long Beach City College,
B.A. Southern California Bible College,
M.A. Southern California Theological Seminary,
D. Th. Southern California Theological Seminary,
D. Th. Denver Charismatic Theological Seminary

Individual Study:
Rabbi Dovid Nusbaum,

Bais Medrash at Yeshiva Toras Chaim,
Hornosteipler Rebbe, Mordicai Tewerski
Group Study:
Rabbi Yaakov Meyer, Aish Denver
Rabbi Yisroel Engel, Director, Colorado Chabad.

Founder:
Jewishpath.org
Jewishlink.net
7commands.com
Bnti.us

Dean of Jewish Studies
B'nai Noach Torah Institute, LLC – Biblical Online Studies

Author of various books.
bnti.us/books.html

Businessman:
Realtor and Property Investor

Other Books By Dr. Akiva Gamliel Belk

A Sincere Journey Ends Without Jesus

This is an autobiography of my spiritual journey. My journey did not begin with the goal of returning to Judaism. My journey began with a desire to give my Baptist Congregation a historical view of Jesus last six days on earth. My journey has been very challenging. If you read this book and if you walk in my footsteps believing in Jesus will become a challenge for you also. The difference is, I returned to Judaism. I can help you understand difficult subjects. The journey of my life can be a great help.

Gematria And Mysticism IN GENESIS

The reader will be introduced to truths not discussed among the religions of the world. Hebrew in the Bible unveils answers to many mysteries. The entire Bible is founded upon Genesis, Exodus, Leviticus, Numbers and Deuteronomy and the truths that flow out of these five books is different than the rest of the Bible. Why? There is a system of Hebrew Letters with which each having a numerical value that form interesting relationships. These number relationships reveal interesting and mystifying Truths within the Hebrew Letters, Words, Phrases etc. of the First Five Books. The cost of this book is a small investment for what the reader will learn.

Mysterious SIGNS Of The Torah in GENESIS

Mysterious SIGNS Of The Torah Revealed In GENESIS is an exploration of Biblical truths organized into the Weekly Parshat Study of the Bible. Dr. Akiva Gamliel has been recording and referencing decades of study and research. He has gathered, compiled and organized years of discovery into this mystical book for us to learn, enjoy and share. Many years can pass between one discovery to another which forms a bridge between two discoveries. Revelations are the product of many bridges. Enclosed in this book are some of these special relationships.

Mysterious SIGNS Of The Torah in EXODUS

This is the second in a series of Five Books, God Willing. This book is deep, intense, inspiring and extremely interesting yet, easy to read and follow.

Dr. Akiva Gamliel includes a Gematria Chart in the beginning of the book. Like each of Dr. Akiva Gamliel's Gematria books there are special Gematrias waiting to be discovered. There is a special sweetness in sharing a Torah Gematria / Sign during a wonderful warm Friday evening Shabbat meal or on another occasion.

Would You Like To Be Jewish ?
Many readers would like to know what it is like to be Jewish. Some have tried to learn what it is like to be Jewish. Some may have visited with a Rabbi who may have said something like this, 'Why do you want to convert? Why do you want to be Jewish? We don't do conversions in Judaism.' You ended up walking away disappointed, angered, exasperated, annoyed and very dissatisfied. This book answers questions about what Jews believe in a way you will not forget.

Would You Like To Be Jewish 2 ?
This is a continuation of the first book, Would You Like To Be Jewish. In this book we learn that God has always had a plan, even before the

beginning of Creation. We learn how God Teaches us to repent when we make mistakes. We discover God is very understanding, compassionate and forgiving. Dr. Akiva Gamliel shares about fallen angels, Satan, hell and how to live eternally with God. This book is a must read for anyone really seeking Truth.

PASSOVER
The LAST SIX DAYS of Jesus Life On Earth

The Gospel Writers each offer a different perspective of Jesus last six days on Earth. They differ some. I offer my own perspective as a Jew that has been on both sides of this discussion. If you are a Christian... If you believe in Jesus, this book will be very challenging. I started on this Journey almost 30 years ago with a desire to give my Baptist Congregation a historical view of Jesus last six days on earth. Since then I have returned to Judaism. I share some untold stories and fill in some of the blank... My journey can be of great help if you discern there are problems with the story Christian Writers tell of Jesus last six days on earth.

Order At:

http://www.bnti.us/books.html

www.ingramcontent.com/pod-product-compliance
Lightning Source LLC
Chambersburg PA
CBHW060519100426
42743CB00009B/1379